CW00418772

The Peacock and the Buffalo

For Tamara

The Peacock and the Buffalo

The Poetry of Nietzsche

Translated by James Luchte

Continuum International Publishing Group
The Tower Building
11 York Road
London SE1 7NX

80 Maiden Lane
Suite 704
New York, NY 10038

www.continuumbooks.com

Originally published as *Nietzsche: Gedichte*, Reclam, Stuttgart, 1986

British Library Cataloguing-in-Publication Data
A catalogue record for this book is available from the British Library.

ISBN: HB: 978-1-4411-1860-8

Library of Congress Cataloguing-in-Publication Data
A catalog record for this book is available from the Library of Congress.

Typeset by Servis Filmsetting Ltd, Stockport, Cheshire
Printed and bound in Great Britain by The MPG Books Group

CONTENTS

INHALT

Benutzte Ausgaben – Bibliographic Sources

K: Nietzsches Werke, Alfred Krönen Verlag, Leipzig, 1919, Bd. VIII.

B: Friedrich Nietzsche. Werke und Briefe, historisch-kritische Gesamtausgabe, hrsg. von H. J. Mette, C. H. Beck'sche Verlags-buchhandlung, München, 1933 ff., Bd. 1 u. 2.

H: Friedrich Nietzsche, Werke in drei Bänden, hrsg. von K. Schlechta, Carl Hanser Verlag, 2. Aufl., München, 1960, Bd. 1–3.

Jugendgedichte (1858–1868)

'Scherz, List und Rache' (1882) (H II, 17–32)

BIOGRAPHY

James Luchte is Lecturer of Philosophy and Programme Coordinator for the MA in European Philosophy at the University of Wales, Lampeter, UK. His other publications include *Pythagoras and the Doctrine of Transmigration*, *Heidegger's Early Philosophy: The Phenomenology of Ecstatic Temporality*, *Nietzsche's Thus Spoke Zarathustra: Before Sunrise* (editor), *Kant's Critique of Pure Reason: A Reader's Guide* (all Continuum). He has also published numerous articles on various topics in *European Philosophy*.

ACKNOWLEDGEMENTS

There are many people I would like to thank for their aid, feedback and support in the completion of this project. Among these are Peter Murray, Christa Davis Acampora; Rainer Hanshe, Yunus Tuncel, and David Kilpatrick of the *Nietzsche Circle*; Babette Babich, Jennifer Anna Gosetti-Ferencei, Graham Parkes, Duncan Large, Arno Böhler, Khalid Al-Maaly, Stephan Koranyi, Jim Urpeth, Mark Sandy, Peter Yates, Uschi Nussbaumer-Benz, Wang Shunning, Laura Hird, David Johnson, and the *Nietzsche Music Project*.

I would like to thank Eva Leadon for her suggestions for an early draft of the first edition of *The Peacock and the Buffalo: The Poetry of Nietzsche*.

I would also like to thank my students in my Nietzsche course, who, over the last few years, have provided much insight and enthusiasm in our readings of Nietzsche's poetry.

On a personal note, I would like to thank my partner Tamara Al-Om for her interest, feedback and support during the work on this Second Edition. I would also like to thank my children, Zoe, Soren and Venus, for their patience, understanding and love.

TRANSLATOR'S NOTE

The Peacock and the Buffalo: The Poetry of Nietzsche is a translation of *Friedrich Nietzsche: Gedichte* (ISBN 3-15-007117-8) from the Universal-Bibliothek, published by Philipp Reclam Jun. Stuttgart. We have supplied the bibliographic sources for this work with the German translation of the poems.

This second edition of *The Peacock and the Buffalo: The Poetry of Nietzsche* contains various new and revised translations of some of the earlier formulations in the first edition. As for the style of the translation in the new edition, the English translation has been laid out, in the manner of Michael Hamburger's translation of the poetry of Hölderlin, in the same compositional structure to facilitate ease in any comparison of the German and English texts. Moreover, there has been a decided attempt to avoid the common practise of forcing the German writer into English idiomatic formulations and, in the case of some of the earlier poems of Nietzsche, English rhyme schemes. This decision was influenced, among other factors, by a reading of an unnamed translation of Heine which, in its effort to supply English rhyme schemes, succeeded not only in nullifying the meaning of Heine's expression, but also of supplying the reader with rather mediocre poetry. In this way, the current translation leans towards a literality which aims to facilitate an attentiveness to the raw meaning of the poems as expressed in German. This is all the more necessary in the case of Nietzsche who, as in all of his writings, took great pains to render his feelings and thoughts into precise – albeit often ambiguous – expressions. Readers may, in this regard, bring their own sense of German and English idiom to a reading of the poems.

PREFACE TO THE FIRST EDITION

They learned their vanity from the sea: is the sea not the peacock of peacocks?

Even before the ugliest of all buffaloes does it spread its tail, never becoming tired of its lace-fan of silver and silk.

Disdainfully the buffalo glances, its soul near to the sand, closer still to the thicket, nearest, however, to the swamp.

What is beauty, sea and peacock-splendor to it! This parable I speak to poets.

Friedrich Nietzsche, Werke in Zwei Bänden, I, p.633

Nietzsche is a poet by instinct – he is driven to it. And, it does not seem to be merely vanity that compels his voice, but an irrepressible desire to express his life and fate – intimately and symbolically – to disclose his *truths* and *delusions*. He told us, after all, that honesty is our youngest virtue. His first poems are naive compositions of feeling, often troubled, surrounding events such as his father's death and his departure from Pforta, exposing, in a raw and deep effluence, his youthful turmoil. He strikes one at times as a Romantic in the manner of Hölderlin's *Hyperion* or Goethe's *The Sorrows of Young Werther*, who can see all too clearly the tragic destination of his life.

At other times, Nietzsche seems to have been troubled by the ambiguity of his poetic 'tic tock' – he is troubled by the seemingly ludicrous eruption of poesy amid his inner experience. His 'gift' is simultaneously 'poison' – it is a gift since it allows Nietzsche to express his truth in honesty. Yet, as a philosopher in the *age of reason*, of Bismarck and Victoria, the poison, infection of poetry would only be seen as a stigma upon his reputation . . . and a question mark over his commitment to 'truth'. Aware of his *timely* predicament, and utterly heedless, Nietzsche digs in for the good fight for poetry and its perspective between heaven and earth. He sets free an array of poetic voices, masks, and larvae, castigating and celebrating – and exploring the habitats of the poet.

There is, for instance, the scoffs of the birds in *Dionysos Dythrambs*,

> Only fool! Only poet!
> Only colorful speaking,
> From a colorful larval fool,
> Climbing upon false broken
> Words and false rainbows
> Between false heavens
> Crawling and creeping –

In *Poet's Profession*, there is a mock inquisition of his own sanity with the question, 'You a poet? Are you right in the head?' The answer, repeated across the poem, exposes not only Nietzsche's attempts to mock, to laugh at his own poetic dilemma, but also expresses his anxiety with respect to the *seriousness* of poetry.

> Yes sir, you are a poet,
> Shrugged the woodpecker.

We can comprehend both his laughter *and* his anxiety if we bring into view the historical fabric of Nietzsche's life and work. For the reductionists and vulgar positivists of the 19th century, any confession of poetry was lettered and quarantined as mere 'enthusiasm'. Kant himself (dutifully following Plato) pioneered this pejorative against his new enemies Jacobi and Hamann, who among others, resisted the coronation of reason as the logical and formal criterion for truth. It seems to be no coincidence that the label 'enthusiast' emerges with Kant's usurpation of the transcendental, creative imagination in the second edition of his *Critique of Pure Reason*. In the wake of the duly deputised *authority* of reason, philosophers such as Hölderlin, Goethe and Schiller became regarded merely as poets – or, worse still, writers – *scribblers*. *Paganism*, *romanticism* and *transcendental naturalism* were exiled from the Blessed Islands of Critical Philosophy and Victorian morality to the future opium dens and absinthe asylums of Nietzsche's day.

The common root of poetry and philosophy is dug up, severed, and put to sleep. The Poets, still convalescing from their suppression under Renaissance Neo-Platonism, were again cast away from the *polis*.

Poetry (*poiesis*) itself was raped, spread out as 'poetry' and 'prose'. 'Mere' poetry was one of the offspring gestated from this rape – a diminished art, serving merely to flatter and console the discrete, divided 'ego' – the other progeny need no introduction.

Poiesis is no longer possible, it was said. Such 'revelation' is *beyond the limits of possible experience* – or conflicts, in its very freedom, with convention and custom. Yet, *modernity* did not break the old law tablets, but put them to *use* as morality. The new law tablets lay abandoned . . .

Nietzsche is an untimely poet-philosopher. If only, one could lament, he had lived earlier, he would have worked amidst *higher men* such as Schiller, Goethe and Lessing, who did not seemingly ascertain any distinction between poetry and philosophy.

Yet, by the time of Nietzsche's emergence, poetry had already been overthrown from its time-honoured status as the fountain of truth. However, that which is significant is that Nietzsche did not suppress this poetic impulse which took hold of him. Nor did he seek an antidote for his poetic 'gift'. Not only did Nietzsche increasingly write in an aphoristic style, but he also included poetry in his published 'philosophical' works.

Nietzsche gives an indication of this coming to terms in his poem *The Wanderer*, where he writes:

> No path any more! Only abyss and deathly silence!
> You wanted this! From the path your will strayed!

Now, wanderer, it was worth it!
Now, look cold and clear!
You are lost, you believe – in danger.

The watershed for Nietzsche's poetry was of course *Thus Spoke Zarathustra* where he takes on – amidst his poetic *topos* – not only the usurpers of the *truth of poetry*, but also the modern poetry of decline, which served merely to ornament the world of logic and science. Zarathustra laments that he is weary of poets who have perversely fulfilled Plato's denunciation of poetry by inscribing their own distance from the difficult path of truth. The latter exiled the poets from the *polis* on the grounds that they lied too much. Yet, with his own Great Lie, he shows himself to be another poet. Yet, Zarathustra celebrates the poet who can lie, as he is the one who can alone tell the truth. After Plato, like Kant, only an implementation of a known script will be tolerated. The official line is born. Plato, weary of time and world, wrote a 'poetry' with the pretence of transcending time, world and life.

Zarathustra seeks, however, to plumb the ugliness, horrors and joys of life and time – and calls on others to find their own tenuous *truths* between the earth and sky. He warns *a Plato* of 'wild dogs barking in the cellars', when he strives for the Heights. Zarathustra himself has no problem confessing that 'poets lie too much'. Yet, he is aware that this question incites very powerful and *dangerous* philosophical questions. Is not the imperishable another of the poet's lies, as well as truth, beauty and goodness? Is there a distinction between 'Good' and 'Evil'? Does not Plato himself draw out a 'divided line'? And, is not Zarathustra also a poet?

Nietzsche's uncertainty with respect to poetry transfigures into a love and affirmation of his gift/curse. In a tribute to the pre-Socratic poet-philosophers, he takes his good fight to Plato and his offspring. Yet, as he is untimely, he beckons the poet-philosopher *of the future* to retrieve the life and fate of *poiesis*. It is the poet-philosopher who will abandon the lies of the imperishable – but for *more plausible* (or more desirable) lies, truths. Nietzsche writes in *Through the Circle of Dionysos-Dithyramben* (103): 'The poet, who willingly and knowingly lies/can alone tell the truth.' It is such a poet who can disclose *makeshift* truths between earth and heaven – *new lies/truths*.

Nietzsche takes Plato to task in the *Preface* to *Beyond Good and Evil* for having denied perspective, and thus life itself. The poet of *tomorrow* will express the play of light and shadow, the erotic and *al-chemical* marriage of life and death, in the topographical language of perspective.

This inextricable marriage of 'high' and 'low' opens up the inexorable significance of life and perspective. After the death of God, a character in a recent poem, there is once again *only* poetry and its uncertainty – this world and its desires. *The world is will to power – and nothing else besides . . .*

Nietzsche takes away the ground *where* we stand – he returns us to the contested truths of poetry, time and world – perspectives amidst life and death. Reason and its ideal is also merely poetry, as with the creative figures of Kantian regulative ideas.

Nietzsche remains a poet – *and* philosopher – for him there can be no contradiction. He continues to write and draw his most powerful themes and insights amid the poetic act. Yet, he does not give it all away. He keeps some of his most radical insights and 'reasons' hidden away in his unpublished poetry. Yet, it is here where we can see Nietzsche, the philosopher of honesty, in his most naked moments. It is in this way that even those who have a great familiarity with Nietzsche's published writings will be astonished and shocked at the raw-ness and radicality of his poetry.

Nietzsche's practise of writing and composition in itself challenges our strict classifications of poetry, aphorism and prose. He wrote in notebooks throughout his life, whether he was in Germany, or later as he moved around between the Alps, Turin and other totemic locations. It is from these notebooks that Nietzsche drew the content of his published works. The trace of a *method* is indicated for us by Nietzsche in his many published works in which poetry and aphoristic text, etc. cohabit single books. Poetry plays an indispensable role in these books, including a philosophical role, as it discloses the *makeshift* status of philosophical inquiry and the impossibility of a unified, logical system of truth. Poetry is not a mere ornament for a 'substantive philosophy', frills for a 'gay science' – it opens up a *topos* for the pursuit of truth. In light of Nietzsche's affirmation of poetry, we are brought face to face with Zarathustra's parable to the poets.

Zarathustra is tired of the poets and their derivatives across time – but, all is poetry, and everyone a poet. He, unlike Plato, who was weary of the world, time and life, is tired of the vanity of *mere* poets – peacocks – who no longer desire truth in its 'love and hate', but who seek to escape existence and life. The eyes on the peacock's tail were placed there, after all, by Hera after the death of Argos. These eyes cannot see, but have only an ornamental significance – indicative of vanity.

The buffalo is disdainful of the self-conceit of the peacock. She abides in the dust of the earth, 'near to the sand with its soul, closer still to the thicket, nearest, however, to the swamp'. The buffalo stands in the background, in uglier regions, a herd animal, she hides in its belonging. Yet, it is precisely across such regions a peacock must traverse to *begin* its difficult pursuit of truth. It must *undergo* much to overcome itself . . . Yet, its vanity keeps it pre-occupied with the wrong lies and the wrong places.

Should one not instead become indifferent to the vanity of the poet, to the peacock, as does the buffalo? Nietzsche writes in 'The poet's vanity,' from *Wit Tricks and Revenge*:

> Only give me glue
> I can find the wood myself!
> The mind in four nonsensical rhymes
> Is not a small object of pride.

The buffalo will care no matter.

Zarathustra is tired of the prevailing poetry of the

'little' self – the ego – the thin froth upon the surface of the raging sea. Such froth disguises the hidden depths, the undertows of the poetry of tomorrow. The froth of the spirit, Zarathustra predicts, will become weary of itself. It too will become a swamp. It will only then become of interest to the buffalo.

Although he is tired of the poets, Nietzsche continues to write a poetry, intimately wedded to his philosophy of existence. In its openness to the ugly, ridiculous and terrible, his poetic philosophy is untimely. It is out of tune with the turn of modern poetic *and* philosophical postures toward the mere ego. As he makes a friend of his poetry, Nietzsche becomes oriented to questions of paradox and existence, 'theological' events and typologies of culture. His own turn toward existence discloses his distance from his contemporaries and evokes the question of the meaning and purpose of poetry itself.

Indeed, in the *Poet's Profession*, he begins to lay out a rough sketch of his poetry-philosophy – when he asks if he is writing poems or setting forth pictures, perspectives. Without answering, we are led to an understanding that poetry is, with Bataille and Heidegger, an intimate hermeneutic, disclosure of existence. The poem intimates and indicates – or, as in his poem *The word* . . . the word *delights* – not as a [realistic] painting or picture, but as a transfiguration and disclosure.

With Nietzsche, poetry and philosophy can once again begin to acknowledge their common root in *poiesis* – and, by *forgetting* that which kept them apart. His gaze upon the *other* of the ego gives Nietzsche access to his own other 'great self' – of body, culture, and the overwhelming powers of life. The 'ego' is just another *makeshift*, another *mask* – in a long line of deception. Its meaning and nothingness is unveiled amid deeper horizons and powers of life and existence.

Nietzsche's poetry intimates a return from Apollo's alleged dream of escape from the earth, his dreamy flight from the raw core of Dionysian life. The sacred *dissolutions* of a discrete 'subject' in death, eroticism and laughter set free the ecstatic self into an openness toward the All, to Being – toward communion *and back*, and to a timely return of this dream image back into the deeper music of life. But, for Nietzsche, this tragedy is recurrently one of joy . . .

Nietzsche's *poiesis* subverts the playing field – *masks* are shattered in the remembrance of their status as mere masks, *makeshifts*. From the perspective of the poet and his uncertainty, all assertions – of *alterity*, *totality* and *purity* – each come crashing down upon the rocks, pulled by powerful, anonymous undertows.

All and each sets forth a story, seeking to mold its desires into wax. There have been many mutations of the wax. Among philosophers and poets, the difference lies in Nietzsche's honesty and his willingness to express our youngest virtue amid uncertainty.

James Luchte
Llanybydder, Wales
2004

PREFACE TO THE SECOND EDITION

> Oh, you wretches who feel all this, who, even as I, cannot allow yourselves to speak of man's being here for a purpose, who, even as I, are so utterly in the clutch of the Nothing that governs us, so profoundly aware that we are born for nothing, that we love a nothing, believe in nothing, work ourselves to death for nothing only that little by little we may pass over into nothing – how can I help it if your knees collapse when you think of it seriously? Many a time have I, too, sunk into these bottomless thoughts, and cried out: Why do you lay the axe to my root, pitiless spirit? – and still I am here.
>
> Hölderlin, from *Hyperion*[1]

That we are still here – and we choose to remain here – amid this apparent nothing – that is the dilemma that the poet-philosopher Nietzsche shares with his childhood hero Hölderlin. It is the honesty of Hölderlin's poetic response to the shattering dilemma of existence which spurs on Nietzsche's own confrontation with the pitiless spirit of time, with the suffocating horizon that encroaches upon this moment of feverish – and ecstatic – life. The honesty of Nietzsche's own poetic response expresses his deep affirmation of a world without pity – and his struggle to bear the greatest weight of the eternal recurrence of the same.

The response intimates his attempt to face this axe that lacerates the root of our being – though not to fall down as a heavy tree, nor to sink into the delusion and sickness of escape – but to fly into the joy of the sky and to perch upon the mountain amid the ice of honesty and truth. It is this creative response that is documented in Nietzsche's poetics of becoming – his courage to face the terrible truth of being, his resistance to the all-too-human, and his convalescence toward the heights of health in the wake of the apparent nothing that surrounds us.

Since the publication of the First Edition of *The Peacock and the Buffalo: The Poetry of Nietzsche*, there has been increasing interest in the more obscure and unknown aspects of Nietzsche's creative work and life. The American release of the First Edition was celebrated on April 23, 2005 with *Transfigurations: Nietzsche's Poetry & Music*, the Inaugural Event of the *Nietzsche Circle* at New York's Deutsche Haus, during which, in conjunction with the *Nietzsche Music Project*, such luminaries as Jennifer Anna Gosetti-Ferencei, David Kilpatrick, and Friedrich Ulfers recited Nietzsche's poetry in German and English. In my own recent work on Nietzsche's poetics, I have continued to attempt to deepen our appreciation of the specific significance of poetry for Nietzsche, and, more generally, of the relationship of poetry (and literature) and philosophy. I have explored the insights expressed in the Preface of the First Edition in 'The Wreckage of Stars: Nietzsche and the Ecstasy of Poetry',[2] 'The Body of Sublime Knowledge: The Aesthetic Phenomenology of Arthur Schopenhauer',[3]

'Zarathustra and the Children of Abraham',[4] and in my edited collection of essays, *Nietzsche's Thus Spoke Zarathustra: Before Sunrise*.[5] The release of this latter work was celebrated in November 2008 with the *International Conference on Nietzsche's Thus Spoke Zarathustra* at the University of Wales, Lampeter, in the United Kingdom.

A usual response to the First Edition – as with Nietzsche's prolific, though seldom heard, musical composition – was one of surprise, if not astonishment.[6] Many – even if they had never read them – seemed to know about Nietzsche's philosophical writings – especially his *The Birth of Tragedy* and *Untimely Meditations* – and his later aphoristic works, such as *Human, All too Human*, *Daybreak*, and *Beyond Good and Evil*, works written after his break with Wagner. Nietzsche was a precocious and prolific writer from the time of his childhood, with extant essays, poetry, and, surprisingly enough, drafts of autobiographies from the earliest years. Yet, the thought that he wrote poetry *as poetry* – and did so throughout his entire creative life – has provoked a curious reaction of disbelief. Of course, the fact that Nietzsche wrote poetry has been quite well known from his published works, not to mention the monumental poesy of *Thus Spoke Zarathustra*. Yet, as he is regarded as a philosopher, such poetic expression has been seen by many readers – especially in the wake of the so-called 'analytic revolution' – as an idiosyncratic flourish of ornamentation that has been met either with a patient indulgence, or with a dry all-too-knowing smile. Nevertheless, the overwhelming importance of poetry to Nietzsche from his juvenilia to the peak of his maturity was not known, much less suspected, even by many of the most widely versed of his readers – including scholars of Nietzsche's 'serious' philosophical works. But, it has become clear from the panorama of his poetic expression that it is poetry (and music) that continued to absorb Nietzsche's energies as the *topos* for his inexorable attempts, as Safranski intimates in his *Nietzsche: A Philosophical Biography*, to self-configure – to incorporate and express – his deep insights into his own lived existence.[7] Indeed, in his review of the First Edition of *The Peacock and the Buffalo: The Poetry of Nietzsche*, Peter Murray clearly specifies the importance – though often the seeming reluctance – of poetic expression for Nietzsche:

> Hölderlin embraces the theme of the poet as the servant of Bacchus, whereas Nietzsche seems to suggest that his poetry is a dubious habit picked up in youth, which he should have grown out of but enjoys too much. Indeed his whole rhetoric concerning songs and singing could be an attempt to justify this pleasure. This ambivalence balances the exhortatory nature of much of Nietzsche's other writing – that which is often found to be 'affirmative'. However, I would like to suggest that it is in the poetry that the affirmative vision is actually formed. The uncertainty expressed in the poetry, coupled with a certain pleasure at the deprecation of self and other, is a more valid expression of

> the requirement for hesitancy and caution that Nietzsche associates with Dionysus than his more strident pronouncements; an expression of the openness which allows the sky to become reflected in the poet rather than become the subject of the poet's vision. It might appear that there is a fine line between lying 'still as a mirror' beneath the 'azure bell', and being the spokesperson of the gods, but Nietzsche's evocation of uncertainty as the basic response to his openness to life differs markedly from the certainty of Hölderlin's response, and Heidegger's interpretation of the poet. Rather than channelling the truth of God or being, the ambivalent role of the philosopher-poet leads to the possibility of an understanding of will to power as being fundamentally a means of negotiating with the resistance to interpretation.[8]

Nietzsche said of himself, in the opening lines of *Daybreak*, that he is a subterranean man, excavating the depths of human experience in his creative work. As I have recently argued, Nietzsche's poetic expression is no mere supplement, nor an attempt to appeal to the baroque aspects of thought which exceed logical, mathematical and scientific expression. Indeed, as I have argued, it is through poetry – and especially *Thus Spoke Zarathustra*, that not only does Nietzsche attempt to overcome the 'theoretical man' as indicated in *The Birth of Tragedy* (a work that should have *sung*), but also to enact his own personal resistance to the spirit – or spirit-less-ness – of his – and our – timely age. It is through poetry – and music – that he not only descends into the depths of existence so as to gain a glimpse of truth in her own domain, but also to open up – and hold open – a creative space for his own convalescence as one who has tirelessly attempted to overcome the nihilism of the Platonic-Christian epoch. That which is disclosed through his poetry, moreover, is the secret narrative of his own development as a thinker, as a poet-philosopher of becoming. Indeed, as is to be expected, his earliest poetry – before the death of God – resembles and enacts a dialogue with his own early influences such as Hölderlin and Goethe. However, as the years are traversed, and his confidence as a poet comes to fruition, there is a marked maturation of his poetic insight and expression which is not merely a footnote to his philosophical work, but intimates the *hidden* Nietzsche – his wild desires and exuberant feelings of freedom and joy, such as those expressed in 'Dionysos Dithyrambs', in which he clearly gives expression to his ecstatic sensibilities of flight beyond the human-all-too-human. Indeed, with the later – and last – poetry, it is clear that Nietzsche has overcome the reluctance of the gift/poison of his poetic tick-tock which he laments – and at which he laughs – in his poem 'The Poet's Profession'. This is all the more the case as – with the growing confidence of his life as a poet – he is not only setting forth his insights in the *form* of poetry, but is also engaging with other poets amid the poetic strategies of echoes, replies and tributes to other poets, as is the case with Hölderlin, his enduring love, and Hafis, the great Persian poet from Shiraz.

This second edition of *The Peacock and the Buffalo: The Poetry of Nietzsche* has been released not only in response to the enthusiastic reception and reviews of the first edition, but also in order to improve the depth and precision of the first provisional attempts. The most obvious change in the second edition is the inclusion of the German text side by side with the English translation. Excepting the German rhyme schemes in some of the earlier poetry, the compositional style and structure of the German original have been replicated in the English, moreover, so as to facilitate a comparison between the two texts – and scrutiny of the translation itself. There have also been new translations of significant amounts of the first edition renditions, not only through new readings, but also in response to suggestions by the various readers of the first edition. Of course, there is still much work to do in the overall project of facilitating the reception of Nietzsche's poetry within the English-speaking world, but it is hoped that this present effort will aid future efforts to allow us to comprehend the depth of significance of the title of poet-philosopher.

James Luchte
Damascus, Syria
2009

Notes

1 Hölderlin, Friedrich (1990), Hyperion and Selected Poems, translated by Eric L. Santer, New York: Continuum

Publishing. This quotation serves the argumentation of the Preface to the Second Edition in its disclosure of the situation of provocation for the poetic response that Nietzsche enacts in his poetics of becoming.

2 'The Wreckage of Stars: Nietzsche and the Ecstasy of Poetry', *Hyperion: On the Future of Aesthetics* (New York, 2007).

3 'The Body of Sublime Knowledge: The Aesthetic Phenomenology of Arthur Schopenhauer', *Heythrop Journal*, Volume 50, Number 2, pp.228–42 (Spring, 2009).

4 'Zarathustra and the Children of Abraham', *Pli: The Warwick Journal of Philosophy*, Volume 20, pp.195–225 and *The Agonist*, Volume 2, Number 2 (2009).

5 *Nietzsche's Thus Spoke Zarathustra: Before Sunrise*, Editor, Continuum Publishing (London and New York, 2008).

6 My own initiation into the music of Nietzsche took place, ironically, in a church in Tampa, Florida in 1993 with a performance given by John Bell Young.

7 Safranski, Rüdiger (2002), Nietzsche: A Philosophical Biography, translated by Shelley Frisch, New York and London: W.W. Norton Books.

8 Murray, Peter (2008), 'The Peacock and the Buffalo: the Poetry of Nietzsche' (review), *The Journal of Nietzsche Studies*, Issue 35/36, pp.204–7 (Spring/Autumn 2008).

Jugendgedichte
(1858–1868)

Poems of Youth
(1858–1868)

Ein Spiegel ist das Leben

Ein Spiegel ist das Leben.
In ihm *sich* zu erkennen,
Möcht ich das erste nennen,
Wonach wir nur auch streben.!!

Zum Geburtstag

Wo die Natur die schönsten Gaben streue
Wo Wald und Berg der Musen Aufenthalt
Wo stets der Himmel mit azurner Bläue
Auf immer grüne Auen niederstrahlt
Wo jeder Tag und jede Stund aufs neue
Des Herren segensreiche Allgewalt
Des ewgen Vaters liebevolle Treue
Ja sein Bild selbst uns unvergänglich malt.
So tönt auch heut ein froher Lobgesang
Empor zum Herren über Tod und Leben
Daß er Dir – ewig sei ihm Preis und Dank
Ein neues Jahr durch seine Huld gegeben.
Mög reicher Segen Dir in ihm erblühen
Und aus des Februares düstrer Nacht
Erhebe sich das Jahr Dir, wie aus Morgenglühen
Die Sonne steigt in wonnevoller Pracht. –

A mirror is life

A mirror is life.
In it, we see *only* ourselves
May I be first to name
Whereafter we also strive.!!

Birthday

Where nature strews her most beautiful gifts
Where muses haunt forest and mountain
Where the sky with azure blue stain
Radiates always upon green meadows
Where upon every new day and hour
Is painted the imperishable image
Of the blissful might of the lord
Of the loving loyalty of the father.
So sound today happy songs of
Praise to the master of life and death
Eternally praise and thank him,
Through his grace, he gave you a new year.
May rich blessings bloom upon you
And from February's dark night
A new year will rise for you, as the morning
Glory of the sun rises in joyful magnificence.

Auf nackter Felsenklippe steh ich

Auf nackter Felsenklippe steh ich
Und mich umhüllt der Nacht Gewand
Von dieser kahlen Höhe seh ich
Hienieder auf ein blühend Land.
Einen Adler seh ich schweben
Und mit jugendlichen Mut
Nach den goldnen Strahlen streben
Steigen in die ewge Glut.

O süßer Waldesfrieden

Erheb mein banges Herz
Das keine Ruh hienieden
Zur Höhe himmelwärts.
Ich werfe mich ins grüne Gras
Und von der Tränen Quelle
Wird's Auge trüb, die Wange naß
Die Seele rein und helle.
Die Zweige senken sich herab
Umhülln mit ihren Schatten
Den Kranken, Lebensmatten
Gleich einem stillen Grab

I stand naked on a cliff

I stand naked on a cliff
And the fabric of night clothes me
I gaze down from this naked height
Upon blooming meadows.
I see an eagle float
And with youthful zest
Strive into golden streams
rising in the eternal glow.

Oh, sweet forest peace

Lift up my anxious heart that
Finds no rest
In heaven's height.
I throw myself into green grass
And from gushing tears,
My eyes become gloomy, my cheeks wet,
My soul pure and bright.
Branches bend down,
Enshroud the sick and
Weary with their shadows
Like a still grave

Ins grünen Walde möcht ich sterben
Nein! Nein; weg mit den herben
Gedanken! Denn im grünen Wald
Wo lustig Vogelsang erschallt
Wo Eichen ihre Häupter schütteln
Da mag wobald
Manch höhre G'walt
An deinem Sarge rütteln
Da kommt der Seelenfrieden
Zu deinen Grab gegangen
Durch ihn kannst da hienieden
Nur *wahre* Ruh erlangen

Die Wolken die in goldnen Bogen
Dich weiß wie Schnee dich rings umzogen
Sie ballen sich im Zorn zusammen
Und senden ihrer Blitze Flammen
Hernieder und der Himmel weint
Daß in der lieben Frühlingszeit
Wo lauten Jubel weit und breit
Er einzig nur zu finden meint
Sich einer nach dem Tode sehne
Und auf dich fällt manch bittre Träne
Und du erwachst
Stehst auf und siehst dich um und lachst

I would like to die in this green forest
No! No; away with such bitter
Thoughts! There in the green forest,
Where merry bird songs resound
Where oak trees shake
Their mighty heads
Soon a much greater power
Will shake your grave,
Peace of soul
Will come there to your coffin
Only through it can you
Attain true peace

Clouds, in golden beams,
Surround you like white snow,
And gather themselves into storm
And lightning flames down to earth
When the sky weeps in lovely Spring
And jubilation resounds far and wide
He is only meant to find
One who longs for death
Such bitter tears fall upon you
And you wake up
And you stand up
And look around and laugh

Was lebet muß vergehen

Was lebet muß vergehen
Die Rose muß verwehen,
Willst du sie einstmals sehen
In Wonne auferstehen!

Das milde Abendläuten

Hallet über das Feld.
Das will mir recht bedeuten,
Daß doch auf dieser Welt
Heimat und Heimatsglück
Wohl keiner je gefunden:
Der Erde kaum entwunden,
Kehrn wir zur Erde zurück. –
Wenn so die Glocken hallen,
Geht es mir durch den Sinn,
Daß wir noch alle wallen
Zur ewgen Heimat hin.
Selig wer allezeit
Der Erde sich entringet
Und Heimatslieder singet
Von jener Seligkeit!

What lives, must pass

What lives, must pass
The rose must fade
Once you would like to see it
Rise again in joy!

Gentle evening bells

Echo across the fields.
It seems to me that no one
Has ever found home
And happiness in this world:
Scarcely wrested from the earth
We turn back to the earth. –
When the bells echo so,
I get the sense that we will
Always wander
To our eternal homeland.
Blessed is he
Who spits out the earth
And from that blessedness
Sings songs
Of his homeland!

Heimkehr

Das war ein Tag der Schmerzen,
Als ich einst Abschied nahm;
Noch bänger war's dem Herzen,
Als ich nun wiederkam.
Der ganzen Wandrung Hoffen
Vernichtet mit einem Schlag!
O unglückselge Stunde!
O unheilvoller Tag!
Ich habe viel geweinet
Auf meines Vaters Grab
Und manche bittre Träne
Fiel auf die Gruft herab.
Mir ward so öd und traurig
Im teurem Vaterhaus
So daß ich oft bin gangen
Zum düstern Wald hinaus. –

In seinen Schattenräumen
Vergaß ich allen Schmerz
Es kam in stillen Träumen
Der Friede in mein Herz.
Der Jugend Blütenwonne
Rosen und Lerchenschlag
Erschien mir wenn ich schlummernd
Im Schatten der Eichen lag.

Homecoming

That was a day of tears
When once I said goodbye
More frightened is my heart
When I now return.
My wandering hopes
Shattered in one blow
Oh, unhappy hour!
Oh, uneventful day!
I wept many times
At my father's grave
And bitter tears
Fell upon the tomb
I became so lonely and sad
In my father's treasured house
I often wandered into
The dark forest,

In its roomy shadows,
I forgot my pains and sorrows
In silent dreams, my heart
Fills with peace and
Sweet dreams of youth
And roses lull me to sleep
As I lay in the
Shadow of the oak tree.

Ihr Vöglein in den Lüften

Ihr Vöglein in den Lüften
Schwingt mit Gesang euch fort
Und grüßet mir den teuren,
Den lieben Heimatsort.

Ihr Lerchen, nehmt die Blüten,
Die zarten mit hinaus!
Ich schmückte sie zur Zierde
Fürs teure Vaterhaus.

Du Nachtigall, o schwinge
Dich doch zu mir herab,
Und nimm die Rosenknospe
Auf meines Vaters Grab!

You, birds in the sky

You birds in the sky
Resonate with your songs
And greet my precious,
My lovely hometown

Larks, take tender
Blossoms for me
And decorate
My precious father's house

You nightingale,
Come down to me
And take rose buds
To my father's grave!

Sage mir, teuer Freund

Sage mir, teurer Freund, warum du so lang nicht
geschrieben?
Immer hab ich geharrt, Tage und Stunden gezählt.
Denn ein gar süßer Trost ist ein Brief vom Freunde
entsendet,
So wie ein sprudelnder Quell durstige Wandrer erquickt.
Viel auch ist mir wert die Kunde von deinem Befinden:
Habe auch ich doch einst ähnliche Wege gewallt,
Habe so Freud wie Leid mit dir zusammen genossen,
Und in Freundesverein wurde das Schwerste uns leicht.
Freilich weiß ich recht wohl: Schuljahre sind schwierige
Jahre,
Nie wird jegliche Last, Mühe und Arbeit gescheut.
Oft auch möchte die Seele sich los von den hemmenden
Fesseln
Reißen, in Einsamkeit flüchten das fühlende Herz;
Aber auch diesen Druck erleichtert die treuliche
Freundschaft,
Die sich stets voll Trost, voll von Erhebung uns naht.
Unter Freunden ist nichts, was der eine dem andern
verbürge;
Alles teilen sie sich mit im vertrauten Gespräch.
Ist auch der eine entfernt, die Liebe durchsegelt die Lüfte,
Und in Gestalt eines Briefs naht sie dem einsamen
Freund.
Teurer! Bald nahet der Tag wo auch wir uns wieder
erblicken,

Tell me, dear friend

Tell me, dear friend, why did you not write for so
long?
Always I waited, days and hours I counted,
A letter from a friend is sweet comfort,
like a
Babbling brook, it quenches a thirsty wanderer.
Very much I would like to hear of your situation:
I once had wanted, after all, a similar path,
To share joy and suffering together with you,
And in friendship make the heaviest light.
Naturally I know: school years are
difficult –
Never would burden, effort and work be shunned.
Often the soul would want to leave
its fetters,
Flee the feeling heart into solitude;
But pressure facilitates true
friendship,
Full of trust and consideration.
Between friends, there is
no secrecy,
Everything is shared in close conversation.
If one is far away, love sails through the air,
In the form of a letter, it nears the lonely
friend.
Dear One! The day draws closer when
we will see

Und des trauten Gesprächs lang schon entbehrten uns
freun.
Aber nur kurz ist die Freud! Denn bald enteil ich von
neuem,
Nicht nach Pforta zurück, wo nur die Strenge regiert,
Nicht nach dem Fichtelgebirg dem düsteren, nein, in die
Heimat!
Ach wohl zum letzten Mal grüß ich den teuersten Ort!
Doch – die Entfernung hemmt nicht der Seelen stete
Verbindung,
Et manet ad finem longa tenaxque fides!

Saaleck

Selger Abendfrieden
Schwebt über Berg und Tal.
Holdlächelnd sendet die Sonne
Hernieder den letzten Strahl.

Die Höhen rings erglühen
Und schimmern in Glanz und Pracht.
Mich dünkt, die Ritter entstiegen
Den Gräbern mit alter Macht.
Und horch! Aus den Burgen ertönet
Lautrauschend ein lustiger Schall.
Die Wälder rings horchen und lauschen
Dem wonnigen Widerhall.

Each other again and happily resume
our long
Missed conversation. But only short will be
our joy!
Then I will return, not back to Pforta where only the
Strong reign, not to the dark pine mountain, no, to my
home!
Though for the last time I will greet the precious place –
Distance does not hinder the soul's steady
union,
Et manet ad finem longa tenaxque fides![1]

Saaleck[2]

Tranquil evening peace sways
Over mountain and valley
The sun sends sweet smiles
Down with its last rays.

The heights around glow and
Shimmer in glory and splendor
One feels that the knights rise
From the grave with ancient power.
Hark! The castle is alive
With merry sound, the
Forest listens and laughs
With the joyous echoes.

Dazwischen erklingen viel Lieder
Von Jagdlust, von Kampf und Wein:
Hell schmettern die Hörner; es schallen
Laut dröhnend Trommeten hinein.

Da sank die Sonne; verklungen
Verhallet der freudige Klang.
Und Grabesstille und Grauen
Umhüllte die Hallen bang.

Die Saaleck liegt so traurig
Dort oben im öden Gestein.
Wenn ich sie sehe, so schauert's
Mir tief in die Seele hinein.

Ohne Heimat

Flüchtge Rosse tragen
Mich ohn Furcht und Zagen
Durch die weite Welt.
Und wer mich sieht, der kennt mich
Und wer mich kennt, der nennt mich
Den heimatslosen Herrn.
Heidideldi!
Verlaß mich nie!
Mein Glück du heller Stern!

Within resound many songs of
Hunting, battles and wine:
Clear horns bellow and
Droning drums resound

The sun sets, the
Merry sounds die away
Stillness and horror
Embrace the anxious hall.

Saaleck lies so sad
upon a barren rock
When I see it
I shudder deep in my soul.

Without a home

Flying horses carry me,
Without fear and timidity,
Throughout the wide world
Who sees me, knows me
Who knows me, names me
The man without a home
Heidideldi!
Do not leave me
My happiness, you bright star!

Niemand darf es wagen
Mich darnach zu fragen,
Wo mein Heimat sei.
Ich bin wohl nie gebunden
An Raum und flüchtge Stunden!
Bin, wie der Aar so frei!
Heidideldi!
Verlaß mich nie!
Mein Glück du holder Mai!

Daß ich einst soll sterben,
Küssen muß den herben
Tod, das glaub ich kaum.
Zum Grabe soll ich sinken
Und nimmermehr dann trinken
Des Lebens duftgen Schaum?
Heidideldi!
Verlaß mich nie!
Mein Glück du bunter Traum.

Entflohn die holden Träume

Entflohn die holden Träume
Entflohn Vergangenheit,
Die Gegenwart ist schaurig,
Die Zukunft trüb und weit.

Nobody would dare
Ask me where
My home *is*
I am not tied
To space and fleeting hours
I am as free as the air
Heidideldi!
Never leave me
My happiness, my gracious May!

That I shall die and
Must kiss harsh death,
I hardly believe.
Towards the grave shall I sink,
Never more to drink from the
Diaphanous foam of life?
Heidideldi!
Never leave me!
My happiness, You, my colorful dream.

The sweet dreams flee

The sweet dreams flee
The past flees,
The present is grim,
The future far and sad.

Ich habe nie empfunden
Des Lebens Lust and Glück
Auf Zeiten längst verschwunden
Schau traurig ich zurück.

Ich weiß nicht, was ich liebe,
Ich hab nicht Fried, nicht Ruh
Ich weiß nicht, was ich glaube,
Was leb ich noch, wozu?

Ich möchte sterben, sterben
Schlummern auf grüner Heid
Über mir ziehen die Wolken,
Um mich Waldeinsamkeit.

Des Weltalls ewge Räder
Rollen im kreisenden Lauf
Des Erdballs rostge Feder
Zieht stets sich von selber auf.

Wie schön, so 'rumzufliegen
Als Luft um den kreisenden Ball
In alle Winkel zu kriechen,
Versiegen im schwebenden All!

Wie schön, die Welt zu verschlingen
In universellen Drang.
Und dann eine Zeitschrift schreiben
Uber den Weltumfang.

I have not found happiness
And the pleasures of life
Sadly I look back upon the
Long passing of time.

I do not know what I love,
I have neither rest, nor peace
I do not know what I believe,
Why do I live, what for?

I would like to die, die
Drowsing in green meadows
Clouds drift over me,
Around my forest peace.

The world's eternal circle
Rolls in circling cycles
The earth's rusty feather
Always races away from itself.

How lovely to fly like this,
A circling ball around the sky,
Crawling into all the spaces,
Drying up in the soaring all!

How lovely to embrace
The world in universal pressure.
And then to write a
New note about the universe.

In meines Magens Schlünde
Zwängt ich Unendlichkeit
Bewies dann durch tausend Gründe,
Endlich sei Welt und Zeit.

Der Mensch ist nicht der Gottheit würdiges Ebenbild

Von Tag zu Tag vertrackter
....
Nach meinem Urcharakter
Gestalt ich mir auch Gott.

Ich wacht von schweren Träumen
Durch dumpfes Läuten auf

My guts churn endlessly
Convinced at last
By a thousand reasons,
That there is world and time.

Man is not God's worthy image

From day to awkward day
....
After my ancient imaginings
Of the shape of God.

Dull sounds wake me,
From heavy dreams

Einsam durch den düsterblauen

Einsam durch den düsterblauen,
Nächtgen Himmel seh ich grelle
Blitze zucken an den Brauen
Schwarzgewölbter Wolkenwelle.
Einsam loht der Stamm der Fichte
Fern an duftger Bergeshalde.
Drüber hin im roten Lichte
Zieht der fahle Rauch zum Walde.
In des Himmels fernes Leuchten
Rinnt der Regen zart und leise,
Traurig schaurig, eigner Weise. –

In deinen tränenfeuchten
Augen ruht ein Blick,
Der schmerzlich, herzlich
Dir und mir verwehte Leiden,
Verlorne Stunden und zerronnen Glück
Zurückrief beiden. –

Lonely, through the dark blue

Lonely, through the dark blue,
Night sky I see
Lightning strike
From brewing black clouds.
Lonely stands the pine tree
Far upon the mountain.
In the red light,
Smoke drifts toward the forest.
In the distant sky lights
Rain falls silently and gently,
Sad, dreadful, in its own way. –

In your tear-stained eyes
Rests a look
Of the pain and heartache
You and I suffered
Recalling our
Forlorn hours and lost happiness. –

Laß mich dir erschließen

Laß mich dir entfalten
Mein verschlossen Herz!
Deiner Liebe heimlich Walten
Ruht so gnadenvoll und mild
Auf meinem kalten,
Welteinsamen Schmerz,
Daß Sehnsucht quillt
In mir nach dir,
Du lichte Himmelskerz!

Laß mich dir erschließen,
Wie mich übertaut
Deines Geistes heimlich Grüßen,
Wenn du auf mich hingeblickt
Zu deinen Füßen
Und mich lieb und traut
An dich gedrückt.
Selig war ich,
Mein Herz schlug mir so laut.

Let me join you

Let me open
My heart to you!
Your secret love,
Merciful and mild
Soothes me through my cold,
Lonely pain,
Longing for you
Fills me,
You bright and heavenly candle!

Let me finally tell you,
How I felt about
Your spirit's secret greeting,
When you caught sight of me
Jumped to your feet
And lovingly
Pressed me close to you.
I was blessed,
My heart was beating loudly.

Jetzt und ehedem

So schwer mein Herz, so trüb die Zeit
Und nie Genügen:
Es zieht mich in den Strudel weit
Wehmut, Schmerz und Vergnügen.
Ich kann den Himmel kaum mehr sehn,
Den maienblauen:
So überstürmen wilde Wehn
Mich jetzt mit Lust und Grauen.

Ich hab gebrochen alter Zeit
Vermächtnis,
Das mir die Kindesseligkeit
Mahnend rief ins Gedächtnis.
Ich hab gebrochen, was mich hielt
In Kindesglauben:
Mit meinem Herz hab ich gespielt
Und ließ es fast mir rauben.

Und was es funden? Hin ist hin!
Nur Tränen!
Die Körner spülte leichter Sinn
Hervor, nicht dumpfes Sehnen,
Die Körner Goldes – war's nicht Schein?
Sie glänzten kurze Weile,
Doch schrieb der Tod ein mächtig Nein
Auf jede, Zeile.

Now and formerly

So heavy is my heart, so sad is time,
And never enough:
It pulls me far into the
Vortex of melancholy, sadness and pleasure.
I can hardly see the sky anymore,
The blue may:
Wild delusions of lust and horror
Storm over me.

I have broken an old time
Legacy,
That calls me to remember
My happy childhood.
I have broken a
Child's oath:
I played with my heart
And was nearly robbed of it.

And where to find it? Gone, is gone!
Only tears!
The grains poured out carelessly
Not like dull strings,
The golden grains – were not illusion?
They shone a short while,
Death wrote a mighty No!
Upon every, every line.

Ich bin wie eine Münze alt.
Vergrünet,
Bemoost, Runzeln auf der Gestalt,
Die einst zum Schmuck gedienet.
Der Zweifel Furchen tief und hart
Darüber gingen,
Des Lebens Schmutz, grau und erstarrt,
Sucht rings sie zu umschlingen.

Und wer mir auch sein Herz geschenkt –
Wohin die Lieben?
Und wer mit Wasser mich getränkt –
Wo sind sie alle blieben?
Und jeder helle Sonnenblick,
Der mich getroffen – ?
Wer nahm den etzten Rest von Glück,
Mein Träumen und mein Hoffen?

Mein zuckend Herz, ich warf es hin
Zu rasten
Und wälzte drüber Lust, Gewinn,
Schmerz, Wissen, Bergeslasten.
Ob es sich quält und drückt und engt –
In wilden Stunden
Da schleudert's flammend und versengt
Empor, was es gebunden.

I am like an old coin.
Green,
Mossy and wrinkled on the form,
That once sparkled like a jewel.
Doubt furrows, deep and hard,
Life's dirt,
Creeps over, grey and frozen,
Seeking to embrace it.

And he who gave his heart to me –
Where are you, dear one?
And, those who quenched my thirst –
Where are they all now?
And, every sun glance
That struck me – ?
Who took the last of my happiness,
My dreams and my hopes?

I put my pounding heart
To rest
And sadness, wisdom, and burden,
Overwhelmed pleasure and profit –
It torments, oppresses and narrows itself,
In wild hours,
It hurls flames and scorches
Triumphant, was it bound.

Und schrieb ich drüber schwarz und dick
Den Blättern
Blieb wenig doch die Schrift zurück
In blutigroten Lettern,
Die Schrift, die auf dem weihen Grund
Ein Gott gezogen:
Der Gott war ich und dieser Grund
Hat sich und mich belogen. –

O daß ich könnte weltenmüd
Wegfliechen.
Und wie die Schwalbe nach dem Süd
Zu meinem Grabe ziehen:
Rings warme Sommerabendluft
Und goldne Fäden.
Um Kirchhofskreuze Rosenduft
Und Kinderlust und Reden.

Dann kniet ich an dem morschen Holz
Ganz stille:
Darüber schwebte hoch und stolz
Der Wolken duftge Fülle.
Der Kirche Schatten hüllte mich,
Die Lilien wanken
Im leisen Hauch und fragen mich
Um meine heißen Gedanken.

And I write upon
Thick black pages
Little remains of the
Blood red letters,
A god wrote
Upon the white ground:
The God was I – reason
Has lied to you and me.

Oh, if I could fly away from
The tired world.
And fly as the swallows to the south
To my grave:
Warm summer breezes
And golden threads.
Rose scents around the churchyard
And childhood pleasures and voices.

Then I kneel in a marsh wood,
Completely still:
Diaphanous clouds
Float over high and proud.
Church shadows blanket me,
Lilies sway and in
Quiet breath ask me
My secret thoughts.

O Ruhe, Fremdling meiner Zeit,
Ich grüße
Dich aus der stummen Einsamkeit,
Wo ich mein Leben büße.
Aus meines Lebens Bronnen quill
In heiligen Fluten:
Ich schau auf dich und lasse still
Mein sehnend Herz verbluten.

Erinnerung

Es zuckt die Lippe und das Auge lacht,
Und doch steigt's vorwurfsvoll empor,
Das Bild aus tiefer, tiefer Herzensnacht –
Der milde Stern an meines Himmels Tor.
Er leuchtet siegreich – und die Lippe schließt
Sich dichter – und die Träne fließt.

Herüber, hinüber
Fliegen der Blicke glänzende Funken,
Trüber und trüber
Wölbt sich mein Himmel, wehmuttrunken,
Lieber, ach lieber
Bräche des Herzens zitternder Grund –

Oh, peace, stranger of my time,
I greet
You from my silent loneliness,
Where I serve penance for my life.
From my life pours forth a
Fountain of holy waters:
I look at you, and quietly,
My longing heart bleeds.

Remembrance

It twitches the lips and the eyes laugh,
And still rises the vision reproachful,
From the deep, deep heart of the night –
The gentle star at my heaven's door.
He lights up triumphantly – and the
Lips close tightly and tears flow.

Over here and over there
Fly the shining flames of lightning,
Gloomy and gloomier
Clouding my sky –
Dear, oh dear,
It breaks the trembling ground of my heart –

Herüber, hinüber
Zucken die Blitze – doch schweiget der Mund.
Wolkensammler, o Herzenskündiger,
Mache uns mündiger!

Ich habe dir und mir vergeben und vergessen;
Weh! Du hast dich und mich vergessen und vergeben.

Noch einmal eh ich weiterziehe

Noch einmal eh ich weiterziehe
Und meine Blicke vorwärts sende
Heb ich vereinsamt meine Hände
Zu dir empor, zu dem ich fliehe,
Dem ich in tiefster Herzenstiefe
Altäre feierlich geweiht
Daß allezeit
Mich seine Stimme wieder riefe.

Darauf erglühet tief eingeschrieben
Das Wort: Dem unbekannten Gotte:
Sein bin ich, ob ich in der Frevler Rotte
Auch bis zur Stunde bin geblieben:
Sein bin ich – und ich fühl die Schlingen,
Die mich im Kampf darniederziehn
Und, mag ich fliehn,
Mich doch zu seinem Dienste zwingen.

Over here and over there
Lightning strikes – silences the mouth
Clouds are gathering, oh, broken heart
Make us humble!

I have forgiven and forgotten you and me;
Woe! If you have forgotten and forgiven me.

Once more, before I go

Once more, before I go
I send my gaze forward and
Raise my lonely hands
To you, triumphant, to you I fly,
In my deepest depth of heart
An altar solemnly dedicated
For all time
His voice will call me from afar.

Then it glows deeply inscribed
The Word: the unknown God:
I am his, even if I stay with
The criminal gang for an hour:
I am his – and I can feel the noose
Pulling me down into battle
I could flee, but I will force
Myself to serve him.

Ich will dich kennen Unbekannter,
Du tief in meine Seele Greifender,
Mein Leben wie ein Sturm Durchschweifender
Du Unfaßbarer, mir Verwandter!
Ich will dich kennen, selbst dir dienen.

I would like to know you, stranger,
You, deep in my grasping soul,
The wandering storm of my life
You, the inconceivable, my relative!
I would like to know you and serve you.

Lyrisches
(1869–1888)

Lyrics
(1869–1888)

An die Melancholie

Verarge mir es nicht, Melancholie,
Daß ich die Feder, dich zu preisen, spitze
Und, preisend dich, den Kopf gebeugt zum Knie,
Einsiedlerisch auf einem Baumstumpf sitze.
So sahst du oft mich, gestern noch zumal,
In heißer Sonne morgendlichem Strahle:
Begehrlich schrie der Geier in das Tal,
Er träumt' vom toten Aas auf totem Pfahle.

Du irrtest, wüster Vogel, ob ich gleich
So mumienhaft auf meinem Klotze ruhte!
Du sahst das Auge nicht, das wonnenreich
Noch hin und her rollt, stolz und hochgemute.
Und wenn es nicht zu deinen Höhen schlich,
Erstorben für die fernsten Wolkenwellen,
So sank es um so tiefer, um in sich
Des Daseins Abgrund blitzend aufzuhellen.

So saß ich oft in tiefer Wüstenei,
Unschön gekrümmt, gleich opfernden Barbaren,
Und deiner eingedenk, Melancholei,
Ein Büßer, ob in jugendlichen Jahren!
So sitzend freut ich mich des Geier-Flugs,
Des Donnerlaufs der rollenden Lawinen,
Du sprachst zu mir, unfähig Menschentrugs,
Wahrhaftig, doch mit schrecklich strengen Mienen.

To Melancholy

Melancholy, do not mock me,
If I sharpen my feather to praise you
And, praising you, sit lonely upon a tree
Stump with my head bent to my knee.
You saw me often, especially yesterday,
In the hot rays of the early morning sunshine:
The vulture screams demands in the valley,
He dreams of the carcass on its deadly path.

You error, wild bird, although
Like a mummy I rested upon my block!
You did not see the eye, that delirium of bliss,
Still roll back and forth, proud and exultant.
And, when it did not reach you on the heights,
Dying in the far away welling clouds,
It sank ever deeper into itself so it could
Brilliantly light up the abyss of existence.

I often sit in the deep wilderness,
Ungraciously curved, bent like a barbarian,
And, I think of you, Melancholy,
A penitent, although in the years of youth!
So happily I sit enjoying the vulture's flight,
And the rolling avalanche of thunder,
You spoke to me, incapable of treachery,
Truthfully, but with terrifying expression.

Du herbe Göttin wilder Felsnatur,
Du Freundin liebst es, nah mir zu erscheinen;
Du zeigst mir drohend dann des Geiers Spur
Und der Lawine Lust, mich zu verneinen.
Rings atmet zähnefletschend Mordgelüst:
Qualvolle Gier, sich Leben zu erzwingen!
Verführerisch auf starrem Felsgerüst
Sehnt sich die Blume dort nach Schmetterlingen.

Dies alles hin ich – schaudernd fühl ich's nach –
Verführter Schmetterling, einsame Blume,
Der Geier und der jähe Eisesbach,
Des Sturmes Stöhnen – alles dir zum Ruhme,
Du grimme Göttin, der ich tief gebückt,
Den Kopf am Knie, ein schaurig Loblied ächze,
Nur dir zum Ruhme, daß ich unverrückt
Nach Leben, Leben, Lehen lechze!

Verarge mir es, böse Gottheit, nicht,
Daß ich mit Reimen zierlich dich umflechte.
Der zittert, dem du nahst, ein Schreckgesicht,
Der zuckt, dem du sie reichst, die böse Rechte.
Und zitternd stammle ich hier Lied auf Lied,
Und zucke auf in rhythmischem Gestalten:
Die Tinte fleußt, die spitze Feder sprüht –
Nun Göttin, Göttin laß mich – laß mich schalten!

You bitter goddess, of a wild nature,
You, friend, love to appear near me;
Threatening, you show me the vulture's path
But you do not show me the avalanche of pleasure.
Murderlust breathes through clenched teeth:
Gain your life through agonizing greed!
Tempting, on the stark mountain rock
The flower longs for butterflies.

Shuddering, I feel I am all of this –
Tempting butterfly, lonely flower,
Vulture, waterfall and sharp ice stream,
Rumbling storms – all glory to you,
You grim Goddess, I bow my head deeply,
Upon my knee, a dreadful groaning praise,
Only for your glory, that I stay steadfast
I long for life, life, life!

Mock me not, evil Goddess, that
I braid you with delicate rhymes.
Shudder when you near, a terrifying sight,
Shiver when you try to reach me, evil right,
And I stammer on, song after song,
And scratch out a rhythmic figure:
The ink flows, the sharp feather sprays –
Now Goddess, Goddess, let me, let me go!

Nach einem nächtlichen Gewitter

Heute hängst du dich als Nebelhülle,
Trübe Göttin, um mein Fenster hin.
Schaurig weht der bleichen Flocken Fülle,
Schaurig tönt der volle Bach darin.

Ach! Du hast bei jähem Blitzeleuchten,
Bei des Donners ungezähmtem Laut,
Bei des Tales Dampf den giftefeuchten
Todestrank, du Zauberin, gebraut!

Schaudernd hörte ich um Mitternächten
Deiner Stimme Lust – und Wehgeheul,
Sah der Augen Blinken, sah der Rechten
Schneidig hingezückten Donnerkeil.

Und so tratst du an mein ödes Bette
Vollgerüstet, waffengleißend hin,
Schlugst ans Fenster mir mit erzner Kette,
Sprachst zu mir: 'Nun höre, was ich bin!'

Bin die große, ewge Amazone,
Nimmer weiblich, taubenhaft und weich,
Kämpferin mit Mannes-Haß und -Hohne,
Siegerin und Tigerin zugleich!

After a nightly thunderstorm

Today, sad Goddess, you are encased,
In shrouds around my window.
Dreadfully, abundant pale flakes swirl,
Dreadfully, haunt the sounds of the deep brook.

I see! With each stroke of lightning,
With the roar of untamed thunder,
With the damp of the valley, you, sorceress,
Have brewed a poisonous deadly drink!

Shuddering around midnight, I hear
Your lustful – and lamenting voice,
I see your eyes blink, see your
Sharp thunderous flash.

You tread upon my deserted bed
Fully armored, glistening with force,
Knocking at my window with a brazen chain,
You speak to me: 'Now listen to what I am!

I am the great eternal Amazon
Never feminine, soft or gentle
A fighter with a man's hate and scorn,
I am conqueror and tiger combined!

Rings zu Leichen tret ich, was ich trete,
Fackeln schleudert meiner Augen Grimm,
Gifte denkt mein Hirn – nun kniee! Bete!
Oder modre Wurm! Irrlicht, verglimm!"

Am Gletscher

Um Mittag, wenn zuerst
Der Sommer ins Gebirge steigt,
Der Knabe mit den müden, heißen Augen:
Da spricht er auch,
Doch *sehen* wir sein Sprechen nur.
Sein Atem quillt, wie eines Kranken Atem quillt
In Fieber-Nacht.
Es geben Eisgebirg und Tann und Quell
Ihm Antwort auch,
Doch *sehen* wir die Antwort nur.
Denn schneller springt vom Fels herab
Der Sturzbach wie zum Gruß
Und steht, als weiße Säule zitternd,
Sehnsüchtig da.
Und dunkler noch und treuer blickt die Tanne,
Als sonst sie blickt,
Und zwischen Eis und totem Graugestein
Bricht plötzlich Leuchten aus –
Solch Leuchten sah ich schon: das deutet mir's.

Where I tread, I trample rings of corpses,
My grim eyes hurl torches,
My brain thinks poison – Now kneel! Pray!
Murderous worm! Madness, fade away!'

On the glacier

Around noon, when summer
First rises in the mountains,
The boy with tired, hot eyes:
There he also speaks,
But we can only *see* his speech.
His breath quivers, like a sick person shaking
In his fever night.
Icy mountains, fir trees and streams also
Give him answer,
But we can only *see* the answers.
The waterfalls, like greetings, spring quickly
From the rocks above,
And stand as white trembling statues,
Longingly there.
And sadder still and faithful looks the fir tree,
As it did at other times
And between the ice and deadly rock
A bright flame suddenly gleams –
Such light, I have seen: it dawns on me.

Auch toten Mannes Auge
Wird wohl noch *ein*mal licht,
Wenn harmvoll ihn sein Kind
Umschlingt und hält und küßt:
Noch *ein*mal quillt da wohl zurück
Des Lichtes Flamme, glühend spricht
Das tote Auge: 'Kind!
Ach Kind, du weißt, ich liebe dich!' –

Und glühend redet alles – Eisgebirg
Und Bach und Tann –
Mit Blicken hier dasselbe Wort:
'Wir lieben dich!
Ach Kind, du weißt, wir lieben, lieben dich!'

Und er,
Der Knabe mit den müden, heißen Augen,
Er küßt sie harmvoll,
Inbrünstger stets,
Und will nicht gehn;
Er bläst sein Wort wie Schleier nur
Von seinem Mund,
Sein schlimmes Wort:
'Mein Gruß ist Abschied,
Mein Kommen Gehen,
Ich sterbe jung.'

The dead man's eyes
Will shine *once* more
When his child embraces,
Holds and kisses him:
Once more, the dead eyes pour out,
The flame of light and speak,
Glowing: Child!
Oh child, you know I love you!' –

And speak here all, glowing – icy mountains,
And trees and streams –
With glances the same words:
'We love you!
Oh, child you know I love you!'

And he,
The boy with tired and hot eyes,
Embraces and kisses him,
Stands ardently,
And he will not go;
Softly, he blows his word like a veil
From his mouth,
His grim words:
'My greetings are my farewells
My comings, my goings
I will die young.'

Da horcht es rings
Und atmet kaum:
Kein Vogel singt.
Da überläuft
Es schaudernd, wie
Ein Glitzern, das Gebirg.
Da denkt es rings –
Und schweigt – –

Um Mittag war's
Um Mittag, wenn zuerst
Der Sommer ins Gebirge steigt,
Der Knabe mit den müden, heißen Augen.

Der Herbst

Dies ist der Herbst: der – bricht dir noch das Herz!
Fliege fort! fliege fort! –
Die Sonne schleicht zum Berg
Und steigt und steigt
Und ruht bei jedem Schritt.

Was ward die Welt so welk!
Auf müd gespannten Fäden spielt
Der Wind sein Lied.
Die Hoffnung floh –
Er klagt ihr nach.

It listens all around
And hardly breathes:
No bird sings.
Flying over,
It shudders
Like the glittering mountain.
There it thinks in rings –
And is silent – – –

Around noon it was
Around noon, when
Summer first rose in the mountains,
The boy with tired and hot eyes.

Autumn

This is Autumn: it will break your heart!
Fly away! fly away! –
The sun crawls upon the mountain
And climbs and climbs,
And rests with each step.

How the world became so withered!
Upon tired straining threads
The wind sings its song.
Hope flees –
He laments her.

Dies ist der Herbst: der – bricht dir noch das Herz!
Fliege fort! fliege fort!
O Frucht des Baums,
Du zitterst, fällst?
Welch ein Geheimnis lehrte dich
Die Nacht,
Daß eisger Schauder deine Wange,
Die Purpur-Wange deckt? –

Du schweigst, antwortest nicht?
Wer redet noch?-

Dies ist der Herbst: der – bricht dir noch das Herz!
Fliege fort! fliege fort! –
'Ich bin nicht schön
– so spricht die Sternenblume –,
Doch Menschen lieb ich
Und Menschen tröst ich –

Sie sollen jetzt noch Blumen sehn,
Nach mir sich bücken
Ach! und mich brechen –
In ihrem Auge glänzet dann
Erinnrung auf,
Erinnerung an Schöneres als ich: –
– ich seh's, ich seh's – und sterbe so.' –

Dies ist der Herbst: der – bricht dir noch das Herz!
Fliege fort! fliege fort!

This is the Autumn, it will break your heart!
Fly away! fly away!
Oh, fruit of the tree,
You shake and fall?
What secret
Did the night teach you,
That icy horror covering
Your crimson cheeks? –

You are silent and do not answer?
Who still speaks? –

This is the Autumn, it will break your heart!
Fly away! fly away! –
'I am not beautiful
– So speaks the star flower –,
But I love man
And comfort humans –

They shall now see the flowers,
And will bow down to me
I see it! And break me –
The memory will
Sparkle in their eyes,
Memory, more beautiful than me
I can see it and so I will die.' –

This is the Autumn – it will break your heart!
Fly away! fly away!

Vereinsamt

Die Krähen schrein
Und ziehen schwirren Flugs zur Stadt [caps ok?]
Bald wird es schnein –
Wohl dem, der jetzt noch – Heimat hat!

Nun stehst du starr,
Schaust rückwarts ach! Wie lange schon!
Was bist du Narr
Vor Winters in die Welt entflohn?

Die Welt – ein Tor
Zu tausend Wüsten stumm und kalt!
Wer das verlor,
Was du verlorst, macht nirgends halt.

Nun stehst du bleich,
Zur Winter-Wanderschaft verflucht,
Dem Rauche gleich,
Der stets nach kältern Himmeln sucht.

Flieg, Vogel, schnarr
Dein Lied im Wüsten-Vogel-Ton! –
Versteck, du Narr,
Dein blutend Herz in Eis und Hohn!

Loneliness

The crows cry
And fly to the city
Soon it will snow –
Comfort to the one – who still has a home!

Now I see you stand there rigidly,
Looking back! For how long already!
What a fool you are
To flee before winter comes into the world?

The world – a folly,
Like a thousand deserts still and cold!
Who that loses,
What you have lost will stop nowhere.

Now you stand there
Cursed to winter-wandering,
Like the smoke,
Searching for the cold skies.

Fly bird, sing your song
Like the Desert-Bird-Tone
Hide, you fool, your
Bleeding heart in ice and scorn!

Die Krähen schrein
Und ziehen schwirren Flugs zur Stadt:
– bald wird es schnein,
Weh dem, der keine Heimat hat!

Der Wanderer

Es geht ein Wandrer durch die Nacht
Mit gutem Schritt;
Und krummes Tal und lange Höhn –
Er nimmt sie mit.
Die Nacht ist schön –
Er schreitet zu und steht nicht still,
Weiß nicht, wohin sein Weg noch will.

Da singt ein Vogel durch die Nacht:
'Ach Vogel, was hast du gemacht!
Was hemmst du meinen Sinn und Fuß
Und gießest süßen Herz-Verdruß
Ins Ohr mir, daß ich stehen
Und lauschen muß – –
Was *lockst* du mich mit Ton und Gruß?' –
Der gute Vogel schweigt und spricht:
'Nein, Wandrer, nein! Dich lock ich nicht
Mit dem Getön –
Ein Weibchen lock ich von den Höhn –
Was geht's dich an?
Allein ist mir die Nacht nicht schön –

The crows cry
And fly to the city:
– Soon it will snow,
Sad for him who has not a home!

The wanderer

A wanderer walks through the night
With a steady step;
He carries with him crooked valleys and
Long scornful mockery.
The night is beautiful –
He marches on and on and does not stop,
Not knowing where his way will take him.

A bird is singing through the night
'Oh, bird what have you done!
Do you hinder my senses and feet
And shower me with sweet refrains
To my ear, that I must
Stand and listen – –
You *tempt* me with tone and greeting?' –
The good bird becomes silent and speaks
'No wanderer, no! I do not tempt you
With my song –
I tempt a little woman with scorn –
Why does it concern you?
Only to me is the night not beautiful –

Was geht's dich an? Denn du sollst gehn
Und nimmer, nimmer stillestehn!
Was stehst du noch?
Was tat mein Flötenlied dir an,
Du Wandersmann?'

Der gute Vogel schwieg und sann:
'Was tat mein Flötenlied ihm an?
Was steht er noch? –
Der arme, arme Wandersmann!'

An die Freundschaft

Heil dir, Freundschaft!
Meiner höchsten Hoffnung
Erste Morgenröte!
Ach, ohn Ende
Schien oft Pfad und Nacht mir,
Alles Leben
Ziellos und verhaßt!
Zweimal will ich leben,
Nun ich schau in deiner Augen
Morgenglanz und Sieg,
Du liebste Göttin!

How does it concern you? If you must go,
And never, never stand still!
Why are you still standing?
What did my flute playing do to you,
You, the wanderer?'

The good bird is quiet and ponders:
'What did my flute melody do to him?
Why does he stand still?
The, poor, poor wanderer!'

To friendship

Hail to you, friendship,
My esteemed hope, this
First morning shimmer!
Ah, without end,
Often seemed my path and night,
All life,
Relentless and hated!
I will live twice,
Now I look into your eyes
Morning glow and victory
You, beloved Goddess!

Campo Santo di Staglieno

O Mädchen, das dem Lamme
Das zarte Fellchen kraut,
Dem beides, Licht und Flamme,
Aus beiden Augen schaut,
Du lieblich Ding zum Scherzen,
Du Liebling weit und nah,
So fromm, so mild von Herzen,
Amorosissima!

Was riß so früh die Kette?
Wer hat dein Herz betrübt?
Und liebtest du, wer hätte
Dich nicht genug geliebt? –
Du schweigst – doch sind die Tränen
Den milden Augen nah: –
Du schwiegst – und starbst vor Sehnen,
Amorosissima?

Die kleine Brigg, genannt 'das Engelchen'

Engelchen: so nennt man mich –
Jetzt ein Schiff, dereinst ein Mädchen,
Ach, noch immer sehr ein Mädchen!
Denn es dreht um Liebe sich
Stets mein feines Steuerrädchen.

Campo santo di Staglieno

Dear girl, who gently strokes
The lamb's soft pelt,
Light and flame shines,
Through your eyes,
You little thing, made to laugh,
You are a darling, far and near,
So pious and gentle of heart,
Amorosissima!

What tore the chain so easily?
Who has saddened your heart?
The one who loved you
Did not love you enough? –
You are silent, but tears are
In your gentle eyes
You are silent – and die from longing,
Amorosissima!

The little brig, called 'The Little Angel'

Little Angel, that's what they call me –
Now I am a ship, once I was a girl,
Ah, but still very much a girl!
I turn love around,
My fine helm.

Engelchen: so nennt man mich –
Bin geschmückt mit hundert Fähnchen,
Und das schönste Kapitänchen
Bläht an meinem Steuer sich,
Als das hunderterste Fähnchen.

Engelchen: so nennt man mich
Überallhin, wo ein Flämmchen
Für mich glüht, lauf ich, ein Lämmchen,
Meinen Weg sehnsüchtiglich:
Immer war ich solch ein Lämmchen.

Engelchen: so nennt man mich –
Glaubt ihr wohl, daß wie ein Hündchen
Bella ich kann und daß mein Mündchen
Dampf und Feuer wirft um sich?
Ach, des Teufels ist mein Mündchen!

Engelchen: so nennt man mich –
Sprach ein bitterböses Wörtchen
Einst, daß schnell zum letzten Örtchen
Mein Geliebtester entwich:
Ja, er starb an diesem Wörtchen!

Engelchen: so nennt man mich –
Kaum gehört, sprang ich vorn Klippchen
In den Grund und brach ein Rippchen,
Daß die liebe Seele wich:
Ja, sie wich durch dieses Rippchen!

Little Angel, that's what they call me –
I am adorned with a hundred flags,
And the beautiful captain
Blows upon my helm,
As the hundredth flag.

Little Angel, that's what they call me –
Everywhere, a flame
Will glow for me, I laugh like a lamb,
I travel my path of desire:
I was always like a little lamb.

Little Angel, that's what they call me –
Can you believe that I can bark like a
Little dog and can throw steam and fire
From my little mouth?
Oh, the Devil is my little mouth!

Little Angel, that's what they call me –
I once spoke some bitter words,
My lover fled
Quickly to oblivion:
Yes, he died from these little words!

Little Angel, that's what they call me –
Hardly listening, I jumped to the ground
From a cliff, and broke one rib,
That my dear soul bent:
Yes, she bends through the ribs!

Engelchen: so nennt man mich –
Meine Seele, wie ein Kätzchen,
Tat eins, zwei, drei, vier, fünf Sätzchen,
Schwang dann in dies Schiffchen sich –
Ja, sie hat geschwinde Tätzchen.

Engelchen: so nennt man mich –
Jetzt ein Schiff, dereinst ein Mädchen,
Ach, noch immer sehr ein Mädchen!
Denn es dreht um Liebe sich
Stets mein feines Steuerrädchen.

Mädchen-Lied

Gestern, Mädchen, ward ich weise,
Gestern ward ich siebzehn Jahr: –
Und dem gräulichsten der Greise
Gleich ich nun – doch nicht aufs Haar!

Gestern kam mir ein Gedanke –
Ein Gedanke? Spott und Hohn!
Kam euch jemals ein Gedanke?
Ein Gefühlchen eher schon!

Selten, daß ein Weib zu denken
Wagt, denn alte Weisheit spricht:
'Folgen soll das Weib, nicht lenken;
Denkt sie, nun, dann folgt sie nicht.'

Little Angel, that's what they call me –
My soul is like a kitten,
Indeed, one, two, three, four and five little jumps,
And then hops into the ship –
Yes, she has quick little paws.

Little Angel, that's what they call me –
Now I am a ship, once I was a girl,
Ah, still very much a girl!
I turn love around,
My fine helm.

A girl's melody

Yesterday, girl, I became wise,
Yesterday, I became seventeen years old: –
Now I look like an ugly old man
Except for my hair!

Yesterday a thought came to me –
A thought? Ridicule and scorn!
Have you had thoughts like that?
An untimely feeling!

Seldom a woman dares to think
The old wisdom speaks:
'A woman shall obey, but not lead;
What she thinks now, she will not follow.'

Was sie noch sagt, glaubt ich nimmer;
Wie ein Floh, so springt's, so sticht's!
'Selten denkt das Frauenzimmer,
Denkt es aber, taugt es nichts!'

Alter hergebrachter Weisheit
Meine schönste Reverenz!
Hört jetzt meiner neuen Weisheit
Allerneuste Quintessenz!

Gestern sprach's in mir, wie's immer
In mir sprach; nun hört mich an:
'Schöner ist das Frauenzimmer,
Interessanter ist – der Mann!'

What she says, I do not believe;
Like a flea, she jumps and stings!
'Seldom does she think
And when she thinks, it is nonsense!'

Ancient wisdom is
My loveliest reverence!
Hear now my newfound Wisdom
Like brand new quintessence!

Yesterday it spoke to me as it always
Speaks to me; and now listen:
Lovelier is a woman,
More interesting – is the man!'

'Pia, caritatevole, amorosissima'

Dich lieb ich, Gräbergrotte!
Dich, Marmor-Lügnerei!
Ihr macht zum freisten Spotte
Mir stets die Seele frei.
Nur heute – steh ich, weine,
Laß meinen Tränen Lauf
Vor dir, du Bild im Steine,
Vor dir, du Wort darauf.
Und – niemand braucht's zu wissen –
Dies Bild – – ich küßt es schon.
Es gibt so viel zu küssen:
Seit wann küßt man denn – Ton?
Wer *das* zu deuten wüßte!
Wie? Ich ein Grabstein-Narr!
Denn, ich gesteh's, ich küßte
Das lange Wort sogar.

Aus hohen Bergen

O Lebens Mittag! Feierliche Zeit!
O Sommergarten!
Unruhig Glück im Stehn und Spähn und Warten: –
Der Freunde harr ich, Tag und Nacht bereit,
Wo bleibt ihr, Freunde? Kommt! 's ist Zeit! 's ist Zeit!

'Pia, caritatevole, amorosissima'

I love you, grotto of the grave!
You, marble liar!
Your scorn always
Makes free'st my free soul.
Only today – I stand, I cry,
My tears flow for you
For you, you image in stone,
For you, you words thereon.
And nobody needs to know –
This image – I kissed it already.
There is so much to kiss:
Since when does one kiss – clay?
Who *could* explain that?
How? I am a Tombstone Fool!
I confess, I even kissed
The long carved words.

On high mountains

Oh, Life's Midday! Festive time!
Oh, Summer garden!
Restless happiness in standing, peeking, waiting:
I wait for friends, day and night, I prepare,
Where are you friends? Come! It is time! It is time!

War's nicht für euch, daß sich des Gletschers Grau
Heut schmückt mit Rosen?
Euch sucht der Bach, sehnsüchtig drängen, stoßen
Sich Wind und Wolke höher heut ins Blau,
Nach euch zu spähn aus fernster Vogel-Schau.

Im Höchsten ward für euch mein Tisch gedeckt –
Wer wohnt den Sternen
So nahe, wer des Abgrunds grausten Fernen?
Mein Reich – welch Reich hat weiter sich gereckt?
Und meinen Honig – – wer hat ihn geschmeckt? . . .

– Da *seid* ihr, Freunde! – Weh, doch ich bin's nicht,
Zu dem ihr wolltet?
Ihr zögert, staunt – ach, daß ihr lieber grolltet!
Ich – bin's nicht mehr? Vertauscht Hand, Schritt, Gesicht?
Und *was* ich bin, euch Freunden – bin ich's nicht?

Ein andrer ward ich? Und mir selber fremd?
Mir selbst entsprungen?
Ein Ringer, der zu oft sich selbst bezwungen?
Zu oft sich gegen eigne Kraft gestemmt,
Durch eignen Sieg verwundet und gehemmt?

Ich suchte, wo der Wind am schärfsten weht?
Ich lernte wohnen,
Wo niemand wohnt, in öden Eisbär-Zonen,
Verlernte Mensch und Gott, Fluch und Gebet?
Ward zum Gespenst, das über Gletscher geht?

Was it not for you that today I adorned
The grey glacier with roses?
The stream searches for you, and longingly pushes
Wind and clouds higher into the blue,
Looking for you like a distant spectacle for birds.

High above, a table was set for you by me –
Who lives so close to the stars,
To the grey distance of the abyss?
My kingdom – which kingdom stretches further still?
And, my honey, who has tasted it? . . .

– There you *are*, friends! – Woe, am I not what
You wanted after all?
You hesitate, astonished – I see that you resent your love!
I – am not myself anymore? Has my hand, my walk and
My face changed? And *what* I am, dear friends – am I not?

Another I became? A stranger to myself?
Did I leap away from myself?
A wrestler who too often conquered himself?
Too often resisted his own strength,
Injured and inhibited by his victory?

I searched where the wind blew coldest?
I learned to live,
Where no one lives, in polar bear zones –
Forgot man and god, curse and prayer?
I became like a ghost, wandering over the glacier?

– Ihr alten Freunde! Seht! Nun blickt ihr bleich,
Voll Lieb und Grausen!
Nein, geht! Zürnt nicht! Hier – könntet *ihr* nicht hausen:
Hier zwischen fernstem Eis – und Felsenreich –
Hier muß man Jäger sein und gemsengleich.

Ein *schlimmer* Jäger ward ich! – Seht, wie steil
Gespannt mein Bogen!
Der Stärkste war's, der solchen Zug gezogen – –:
Doch wehe nun! Gefährlich ist *der* Pfeil,
Wie *kein* Pfeil, – fort von hier! Zu eurem Heil! . . .

Ihr wendet euch? – O Herz, du trugst genung,
Stark blieb dein Hoffen:
Halt *neuen* Freunden deine Türen offen!
Die alten laß! Laß die Erinnerung!
Warst einst du jung, jetzt – bist du besser jung!

Was je uns knüpfte, *einer* Hoffnung Band –
Wer liest die Zeichen,
Die Liebe einst hineinschrieb, noch, die bleichen?
Dem Pergament vergleich ich's, das die Hand
Zu fassen *scheut* – ihm gleich verbräunt, verbrannt.

Nicht Freunde mehr, das sind – wie nenn ich's doch? –
Nur Freunds-Gespenster!
Das klopft mir wohl noch nachts an Herz und Fenster,
Das sieht mich an und spricht: 'wir *waren's* doch?
– O welkes Wort, das einst wie Rosen roch!

– Dear old friends! See! Now you look pale,
Full of love and horror!
No, go! Do not delay! Here – you cannot live:
Here between rock and ice –
Here one must be a hunter and a chamois.[3]

I have become a wild hunter! See, how tight
I string my bow!
Only the strongest could pull such a bow – –:
Beware! Dangerous is the arrow
As *no* arrow – away from here! To your salvation! . . .

You turn around? Oh, heart, you carried enough,
Your hope stayed strong:
Open your doors to *new* friends!
Leave the old! Leave your memories!
You were young once, now – you are younger!

Whatever tied us as *a* hopeful band –
Who still reads the pale signs,
That love once wrote?
It is like parchment the hand is too *shy* to touch –
It equally browns, burns.

Are there no more friends – as I call them?
Only ghost friends!
That knock on my heart and window at night,
Look at me and speak: 'It was *us*, after all?'
– Oh, faded word that once smelled like roses!

O Jugend-Sehnen, das sich mißverstand!
Die ich ersehnte,
Die ich mir selbst verwandt-verwandelt wähnte.
Daß *alt* sie wurden, hat sie weggebannt:
Nur wer sich wandelt, bleibt mit mir verwandt

O Lebens Mittag! Zweite Jugendzeit!
O Sommergarten!
Unruhig Glück im Stehn und Spähn und Warten!
Der Freunde harr ich, Tag und Nacht bereit,
Der *neuen* Freunde! Kommt! 's ist Zeit! 's ist Zeit.'

Dies Lied ist aus – der Sehnsucht süßer Schrei
Erstarb im Munde:
Ein Zaubrer tat's, der Freund zur rechten Stunde,
Der Mittags-Freund – nein! fragt nicht, wer es sei –
Um Mittag war's, da wurde Eins zu Zwei . . .

Nun feiern wir, vereinten Siegs gewiß,
Das Fest der Feste:
Freund Zarathustra kam, der Gast der Gaste!
Nun lacht die Welt, der grause Vorhang riß,
Die Hochzeit kam für Licht und Finsternis . . .

Oh, youthful visions that misunderstood themselves!
I realized that
I had to change what had become
Old if I wanted to stay related to myself:
Only he who changes himself will stay related to me.

Oh, Life's Midday! Second youth!
Oh, Summer garden!
Restless happiness in standing, peeking and waiting!
I wait for friends, day and night I prepare,
The *new* friend! Come! It is time! It is time!

This song is over – the sweet cry of longing
Died in my mouth:
A magician did this, a friend at the right hour
The noontime friend – No! Do not ask who it was –
It was around noon, and one became two . . .

Now we celebrate inexorable victory,
The feast of feasts:
Friend, Zarathustra comes, the guest of all guests!
Now the world is laughing, the dread curtain is rent,
The wedding day has come for light and darkness . . .

O Mensch! Gib acht!

O Mensch! Gib acht!
Was spricht die tiefe Mitternacht?
‘Ich schlief, ich schlief –,
Aus tiefem Traum; bin ich erwacht: –
Die Welt ist tief,
Und tiefer als der Tag gedacht.
Tief ist ihr Weh – –,
Lust – tiefer noch als Herzeleid:
Weh spricht: Vergeh!
Doch alle Lust will Ewigkeit –,
– will tiefe, tiefe Ewigkeit!’

Oh man, take care!

O man, take care!
What did the deep Midnight say:
'I sleep, I sleep –,
From deep dreams, I awake: –
The world is deep,
And deeper than the day thought.
Deep is her sorrow –
Joy – deeper still than heartache:
Suffering speaks: Pass away!
All joy wants eternity –
– Wants deep, deep eternity!'

An Hafis

Trinkspruch, Frage eines Wassertrinkers

Die Schenke, die du dir gebaut,
ist größer als jedes Haus,
Die Tränke, die du drin gebraut,
die trinkt die Welt nicht aus.
Der Vogel, der einst Phönix war,
der wohnt bei dir zu Gast,
Die Maus, die einen Berg gebar,
die – bist du selber fast!
Bist alles und keins, bist Schenke und Wein,
bist Phönix, Berg und Maus,
Fällst ewiglich in dich hinein,
fliegst ewig aus dir hinaus –
Bist aller Höhen Versunkenheit,
bist aller Tiefen Schein,
Bist aller Trunkenen Trunkenheit
– wozu, wozu *dir* – Wein?

Musik des Südens

Nun wird mir alles noch zuteil,
Was je mein Adler mir erschaute
– Ob manche Hoffnung schon vergraute –:
Es sticht dein Klang mich wie ein Pfeil,
Der Ohren und der Sinne Heil,
Das mir vom Himmel niedertaute.

To Hafis[4]

A drinking verse, or a water drinker's question

The inn that you built,
Is greater than any house,
The drinks that you brewed,
The world could never drink.
The bird, who once was a Phoenix,
Lives with you, as a guest,
The mouse, who gave birth to a mountain,
Who – is almost like you!
You are all and nothing, are the inn and the wine,
Phoenix, mountain and mouse,
You always withdraw into yourself
You always fly out of your self –
You are the height of gloom,
You are all deep illusions,
You are all drunken drinkers,
– What for, why wine for you?

Music of the South

What my eagle promised,
Will still be granted to me –
– If hope already dawns –:
Your sound stings me like an arrow,
The buzz and sensuous salvation
That fell upon me from the sky.

O zögre nicht, nach südlichen Geländen,
Glückselgen Inseln, griechischem Nymphen-Spiel
Des Schiffs Begierde hinzuwenden –
Kein Schiff fand je ein schöner Ziel!

An der Brücke stand

An der Brücke stand jüngst ich in brauner Nacht.
Fernher kam Gesang;
goldener Tropfen quoll's
über die zitternde Fläche weg.
Gondeln, Lichter, Musik –
trunken schwamm's in die Dämmrung hinaus . . .

Meine Seele, ein Saitenspiel,
sang sich, unsichtbar berührt,
heimlich ein Gondellied dazu,
zitternd vor bunter Seligkeit.
– Hörte jemand ihr zu?

Oh, hesitate not toward Southern shores,
Blissful Islands, Grecian nymphs at play
Ships steering toward desire –
No ship has yet found a lovelier destination!

I stand on a bridge

I stood recently upon a bridge in the brown night.
From afar came a song;
Golden drops swell
Over the trembling surface.
Gondolas, light, music –
Drunkenly swim into the dawn . . .

My soul, a stringed game,
Sings to itself, plucks invisibly,
A homely gondola song,
Trembles with colorful happiness.
– Was anyone listening?

Drei Bruchstücke

Glück, o Glück, du schönste Beute!
Immer nah, nie nah genung,
Immer morgen, nur nicht heute, –
Ist dein Jäger dir zu jung?
Bist du wirklich Pfad der Sünde,
        Aller Sünden
Lieblichste Versündigung?

Fern brummt der Donner übers Land,
Der Regen tropft und tropft:
Geschwätzig früh schon, der Pedant.
Dem nichts das Maul mehr stopft.
Kaum schielt der Tag durchs Fenster mir
Und schon die Litanei!
Das predigt, plätschert für und für,
Wie alles – eitel sei!

Der Tag klingt ab, es gilbt sich Glück und Licht,
Mittag ist ferne.
Wie lange noch? Dann kommen Mond und Sterne
Und Wind und Reif: nun säum ich länger nicht,
Der Frucht gleich, die ein Hauch vom Baume bricht.

Three broken pieces

Happiness, oh happiness, you beautiful bounty!
Always near, never near enough,
Always tomorrow, only not today, –
Is your hunter too young for you?
Are you really the path of sin,
All sins
Are lovingly forgiven?

Far away the thunder roars across the land,
Raindrops fall and fall:
The pedant chatters
Already, and nothing will shut his mouth!
The day hardly blinks through my window,
And already he preaches!
And chatters on and on,
Like everyone, in vain!

The day draws on, luck and love fade,
Midday is far away.
How much longer? Then comes the moon and stars
And the wind and frost: I must delay no longer – like the fruit
Which breaks from the tree with a breath.

Spruchhaftes (1869–1888)

Sayings
(1869–1888)

In Basel steh ich unverzagt

In Basel steh ich unverzagt
Doch einsam da – Gott sei's geklagt.
Und schrei ich laut: Homer! Homer!
So macht das jedermann Beschwer.
Zur Kirche geht man und nach Haus
Und lacht den lauten Schreier aus.

Jetzt kümmr' ich mich nicht mehr darum:
Das allerschönste Publikum
Hört mein homerisches Geschrei
Und ist geduldig still dabei.
Zum Lohn für diesen Überschwank
Von Güte hier gedruckten Dank.

Unter Freunden

Ein Nachspiel

1.

Schön ist's, miteinander schweigen,
Schöner, miteinander lachen, –
Unter seidenem Himmels-Tuche
Hingelehnt zu Moos und Buche
Lieblich laut mit Freunden lachen
Und sich weiße Zähne zeigen.

Undaunted, I stood in Basel

Undaunted, I stood in Basel
Alone I stood there, God have pity.
I shouted loudly: Homer! Homer!
And so burdened everyone.
They go to church and back home
And laugh at the loud crier.

I am not bothered by it anymore:
This beautiful audience hears my
Homeric cries and
Indulges me.
As a reward for this exuberance
Of goodness, my printed thanks.

Amongst friends

A play

1.

It is lovely to be silent together
But lovelier to laugh together, –
Under silken skies leaning
Upon moss and beech tree
Lovingly laugh loudly with friends
Show each other gleaming white teeth.

Macht' ich's gut, so wolle wir schweigen;
Macht' ich's schlimm –, so wolln wir lachen
Und es immer schlimmer machen,
Schlimmer machen, schlimmer lachen,
Bis wir in die Grube steigen.

Freunde! Ja! So soll's geschehn
Amen! Und auf Wiedersehn!

2.

Kein Entschuldgen! Kein Verzeihen!
Gönnt ihr Frohen, Herzens-Freien
Diesem unvernünftgen Buche
Ohr und Herz und Unterkunft!
Glaubt mir, Freunde, nicht zum Fluche
Ward mir meine Unvernunft!

Was *ich* finde, was *ich* suche –,
Stand das je in einem Buche?
Ehrt in mir die Narren-Zunft!
Lernt aus diesem Narrenbuche,
Wie Vernunft kommt – 'zur Vernunft'!

Also, Freunde, soll's geschehn? –
Amen! Und auf Wiedersehn!

If I do it well, we will keep silent;
If I do it badly – then we will laugh
And it will always become worse,
Much worse, worse laughter,
Until we climb into the grave.

Friends! Yes! Will it happen like that?
Amen! Good bye!

2.

No apologies! No forgiveness!
Lend an ear, heart and shelter
To this foolish book
You happy, free-hearts!
Believe me, friends,
Do not curse my foolishness!

What *I* find, what *I* seek . . .
Stands there already in a book?
I learned from this foolish book
Initiated into the Fool's-Guild
How reason comes, – 'to reason'!

Well, friends, will it happen like that?
Amen and Goodbye.

Pinie und Blitz

Hoch wuchs ich über Mensch und Tier;
Und sprech ich – niemand spricht mit mir.

Zu einsam wuchs ich und zu hoch –
Ich warte: worauf wart ich doch?

Zu nah ist mir der Wolken Sitz,
Ich warte auf den ersten Blitz.

Baum im Herbst

Was habt ihr plumpen Tölpel mich gerüttelt,
Als ich in seliger Blindheit stand:
Nie hat ein Schreck grausamer mich geschüttelt,
– Mein Traum, mein goldner Traum entschwand!

Naschbären ihr mit Elefanten-Rüsseln,
Macht man nicht höflich erst: Klopf! Klopf?
Vor Schrecken warf ich euch die Schüsseln
Goldreifer Früchte-an den Kopf.

Pine and lightning

I wax high over humans and animals;
And I speak – no one speaks with me.

Too lonely I grew and much too high –
I wait – what do I wait for?

Too close I am to the seat of the clouds, –
I wait for the first lightning.

Tree in autumn

Why have you clumsy oafs shaken me,
As I stood in blissful blindness:
Nothing ever shook me so cruelly
My dream, my golden dream has disappeared!

You are nibbling bears, with elephant trunks,
Must one not first politely: Knock! Knock?
In fright, I threw the bowl of golden fruit
To you – at your head.

Unter Feinden

Nach einem Zigeuner-Sprichwort

Dort der Galgen, hier die Stricke
Und des Henkers roter Bart,
Volk herum und giftge Blicke –
Nichts ist neu dran meiner Art!
Kenne dies aus hundert Gängen,
Schrei's euch lachend ins Gesicht:
'Unnütz, unnütz, mich zu hängen!
Sterben? Sterben kann ich nicht!'
Bettler ihr! Denn euch zum Neide
Ward mir, was ihr – nie erwerbt:
Zwar ich leide, zwar ich leide –
Aber *ihr* – *ihr* sterbt, *ihr* sterbt!
Auch nach hundert Todesgängen
Bin ich Atem, Dunst und Licht –
'Unnütz, unnütz, mich zu hängen!
Sterben? Sterben kann ich nicht!'

'Der Wanderer und sein Schatten'

Ein Buch

Nicht mehr zurück? Und nicht hinan?
Auch für die Gemse keine Bahn?

So wart ich hier und fasse fest,
Was Aug und Hand mich fassen läßt!

Amongst enemies

A gypsy verse

There is the gallows, here is the rope
And the hangman's red beard,
People all round and poisonous looks –
Nothing is new to me!
I know this, after a hundred attempts,
Laughing! I scream in your face!
'It is useless, useless to hang me!
Die? I cannot die!'
You beggars! To your envy, I became
What you – never achieved:
I suffer indeed, I suffer indeed –
But *you* – *you* will die, *you* will die!
Amidst a hundred trips to death
I am breath, vapor and light –
'It is useless, useless to hang me!
Die? I cannot die!'

'The wanderer and his shadow'

A book

Not to go back? Not to ascend?
No path for the chamois?

So here I wait and hold fast,
Where eye and hand holds onto me!

Fünf Fuß breit Erde, Morgenrot,
Und *unter* mir – Welt, Mensch und Tod!

Zu 'Menschliches Allzumenschliches'

1.

Seit dies Buch mir erwuchs, quält Sehnsucht mich und
Beschämung,
Bis solch Gewächs dir einst reicher und schöner erblüht.
Jetzt schon kost ich des Glücks, daß ich dem Größeren
nachgeh,
Wenn er des goldnen Ertrags eigener Ernten sich freut.

2.

Ist von Sorrentos Duft nichts hängenblieben?
Ist alles wilde, kühle Bergnatur?
Kaum herbstlich sonnenwarm und ohne Lieben?
So ist ein Teil von mir im Buche nur:
Den bessern Teil, ihn bring ich zum Altar
Für sie, die Freundin, Mutter, Arzt mir war.

At dawn, the earth is five feet wide,
And under me – world, man and death!

'Human, all too human'

1.

Since this book grew on me, longing and shame
Tormented me,
Until such foliage, rich and lovely, would bloom once for you.
Now I already pay the price for the happiness in my pursuit
Of greatness,
When it hopes for the unexpected yield of a golden harvest.

2.

Does the fragrance of Sorrento not remain?
Is all this wild and cool mountain nature?
Barely autumnal sun and without love?
There is only one part of me in the book:
I will bring the better part to the altar
For you, Friend, who was mother and doctor to me.

3.

Freundin! Der sich vermaß, dich dem Glauben ans Kreuz
zu entreißen,
Schickt dir dies Buch: doch er selbst macht vor dem Buche
ein Kreuz.

Wer viel einst zu verkünden hat

Wer viel einst zu verkünden hat,
Schweigt viel in sich hinein:
Wer einst den Blitz zu zünden hat,
Muß lange – Wolke sein.

In ein Exemplar der 'Fröhlichen Wissenschaft'

Freundin, sprach Columbus, traue
Keinem Genuesen mehr!
Immer starrt er in das Blaue
Fernstes zieht ihn allzusehr!
Wen er liebt, den lockt er gerne
Weit hinaus in Raum und Zeit, –
Über uns glänzt Stern bei Sterne
Um uns braust die Ewigkeit.

3.

Friend! He who presumed to destroy your belief in
the cross,
Sends this book to you: he himself made before this book
the cross.

He who once promised much

He who once promised much
Is silent in himself.
He who once ignited lightning
Must long – be a cloud.

An example of 'joyful wisdom'

Friend, spoke Columbus,
Do not trust pleasure anymore!
He who always stares into the blue
Distance is tempted to see all!
Whom he loves, he gladly lures
Far away into space and time, –
Above us stars shine near stars
All around us roars eternity.

'Die fröhliche Wissenschaft'

Dies ist kein Buch: was liegt an Büchern!
An diesen Särgen und Leichentüchern!
Vergangnes ist der Bücher Beute:
Doch hierin lebt ein ewig *Heute*.

Dies ist kein Buch: was liegt an Büchern!
Was liegt an Särgen und Leichentüchern!
Dies ist ein Wille, dies ist ein Versprechen,
Dies ist ein letztes Brücken-Zerbrechen,
Dies ist ein Meerwind, ein Anker-Lichten,
Ein Räder-Brausen, ein Steuer-Richten;
Es brüllt die Kanone, weiß dampft ihr Feuer,
Es lacht das Meer, das Ungeheuer!

Vorsicht: Gift!

Wer hier nicht lachen kann, soll hier nicht lesen!
Denn, lacht er nicht, packt ihn 'das böse Wesen'.

Seine Gesellschaft zu finden wissen

Mit Witzbolden ist gut witzeln:
Wer kitzeln will, ist leicht zu kitzeln.

'The joyful wisdom'

This is not a book: what matters books!
These coffins and shrouds!
The past is a book's bounty:
Herein lives an eternal *today*.

This is not a book, what matters books!
What matters coffins and shrouds!
This is a will, this is a promise,
This is a last breaking of bridges,
This is a sea wind, an anchor light,
A roaring wheel, a steering right;
The canon roars, her fire like white steam
The sea is laughing, the Monster!

Attention: Poison!

Who cannot laugh here, shall not read here!
If he does not laugh, the 'evil being' will seize him.

Wisdom regarding the right company

It is good to joke with buffoons:
It is easy to titillate one who wants to tickle.

Aus der Tonne des Diogenes

'Notdurft ist billig, Glück ist ohne Preis:
Drum sitz ich statt auf Gold auf meinem Steiß.'

Lebensregeln

Das Leben gern zu leben,
Mußt du darüberstehn!
Drum lerne dich erheben!
Drum lerne – abwärts sehn!

Den edelsten der Triebe
Veredle mit Bedachtung:
Zu jedem Kilo Liebe
Nimm ein Gran Selbstverachtung.

Desperat

Fürchterlich sind meinem Sinn
Spuckende Gesellen!
Lauf ich schon, wo lauf ich hin?
Spring ich in die Wellen?

From the barrel of Diogenes

'Poverty is cheap, happiness is without price:
Instead of sitting on gold, I sit on my rump.'

The rules of life

To enjoy life,
You must stand above it!
That is why you must learn to rise!
That is why you must learn to look down!

The nobility of impulse
Is cultivated advisedly:
For each kilo of love,
Take a gram of self-contempt.

Desperate

Awful to my sense are
Companions who split!
I already run, where do I run?
Do I jump into the waves?

Alle Münder stets gespitzt,
Gurgelnd alle Kehlen,
Wand und Boden stets bespritzt –
Fluch auf Speichelseelen!

Lieber lebt ich schlecht und schlicht
Vogelfrei auf Dächern,
Lieber unter Diebsgezücht,
Eid- und Ehebrechern!

Fluch der Bildung, wenn sie speit!
Fluch dem Tugendbunde!
Auch die reinste Heiligkeit
Trägt nicht Gold im Munde.

Das Wort

Lebendgem Worte bin ich gut:
Das springt heran so wohlgemut,
Das grüßt mit artigem Genick,
Ist lieblich selbst im Ungeschick,
Hat Blut in sich, kann herzhaft schnauben,
Kriecht dann zum Ohre selbst dem Tauben,
Und ringelt sich und flattert jetzt,
Und was es tut – das Wort ergetzt.

Their mouths always spit,
Their throats are gurgling,
Wall and floor always splashed –
Curse upon spittle souls!

I prefer to live bad and simple
Free as a bird upon the rooftops,
I prefer to live amongst thieves,
And oath and marriage breakers!

Curse to culture, when she spews!
Curse to the land of virtue!
Not even the purest holiness
Wears gold in her mouth.

The word

Lively words suit me well:
They jump along so easily,
They greet me with a friendly nod,
They love even in their clumsiness,
Full of blood, they snort most heartily,
Creep slowly to a pigeon's ear,
And now curl and flutter,
And what it does – the word *delights*.

Doch bleibt das Wort ein zartes Wesen,
Bald krank und aber bald genesen.
Willst ihm sein kleines Leben lassen,
Mußt du es leicht und zierlich fassen,
Nicht plump betasten und bedrücken,
Es stirbt oft schon an bösen Blicken –
Und liegt dann da, so ungestalt,
So seelenlos, so arm und kalt,
Sein kleiner Leichnam arg verwandelt,
Von Tod und Sterben mitßgehandelt.

Ein totes Wort – ein häßlich Ding,
Ein klapperdürres Kling-Kling-Kling.
Pfui allen häßlichen Gewerben,
An denen Wort und Wörtchen sterben!

Der Einsiedler spricht

Gedanken *haben*? Gut! sie wollen mich zum Herrn.
Doch sich Gedanken *machen* – das verlernt ich gern!
Wer sich Gedanken wacht – den haben *sie*,
Und dienen will ich nun und nie.

The word remains a tender being,
Now sick, now it convalesces,
Let it have its little life,
Hold it light and tenderly,
Do not clumsily touch and trouble it,
Often it dies from evil looks –
And lies there unformed,
Soulless, poor and cold,
Its little corpse so transformed,
Mishandled by death and dying.

A deathly word – an ugly thing,
A silly kling-kling-kling.
Shame on all the hateful trade,
On whom words and little words will die!

The hermit speaks

You *have* thoughts? Good! You want me to master.
But to *make* thoughts – I willingly forget!
Who made his own thoughts – who has *her*,
I will serve now and never.

Alle ewigen Quell-Bronnen

Alle ewigen Quell-Bronnen
Quellen ewig hinan:
Gott selbst – hat er je begonnen?
Gott selbst – fängt er immer an?

Entschluß

Will weise sein, weil's *mir* gefällt,
Und nicht auf fremden Ruf.
Ich lobe Gott, weil Gott die Welt
So dumm als möglich schuf.

Und wenn ich selber meine Bahn
So krumm als möglich lauf –
Der Weiseste fing damit an,
Der Narr – hört damit auf.

Der Halkyonier

So sprach ein Weib voll Schüchternheit
Zu mir im Morgenschein:
'Bist schon du selig vor Nüchternheit,
Wie selig wirst du – trunken sein!'

All eternal brooks

All eternal brooks
Flow eternally:
And God himself – did he once begin?
God himself – does he always begin?

Resolution

I will be wise because it pleases me,
Not because of some strange call.
I praise God, because God created
The world as foolishly as possible.

I run my way
As crooked as possible –
The wisest is caught by it,
The fool is touched by it.

The rascal

Thus spoke a shy woman to me
At dawn:
'You are already blessed when you are sober,
How blessed will you be – when you are drunk?'

Sieben Weibs-Sprüchlein

Wie die längste Weile fleucht, kommt ein Mann zu uns
gekreucht!

Alter, ach! und Wissenschaft gibt auch schwacher Tugend
Kraft.

Schwarz Gewand und Schweigsamkeit kleidet jeglich
Weib – gescheit.

Wem im Glück ich dankbar bin? Gott! – und meiner
Schneiderin.

Jung: beblümtes Höhlenhaus. Alt: ein Drache fährt
heraus.

Edler Name, hübsches Bein, Mann dazu: o wär *er* mein!

Kurze Rede, langer Sinn – Glatteis für die Eselin!

Das neue Testament

Dies das heiligste Gebet-,
Wohl- und Wehe-Buch?
– Doch an seiner Pforte steht
Gottes Ehebruch!

The seven wives' speeches

After the longest time, a man comes to us
                    Crawling!

Oh aged one! Wisdom gives strength to weak
                    Virtue.

A black gown and silence dresses each
                    Wife – cleverly.

Who shall I thank for my happiness? God! – and my
                    Dressmaker's shop.

Youth: a flowered hollow house. Age: a dragon
                    Coming out.

Noble name, lovely leg, a man included: Oh, would that
  he be mine!

Few words and a longing mind – slippery ice for a little ass!

The New Testament

Is this a holy prayer –
This cheerful and suffering book?
– At its gate stands
The adultery of God!

Einstmals – ich glaub, im Jahr des Heiles Eins

Einstmals – ich glaub, im Jahr des Heiles Eins –
Sprach die Sibylle, trunken sonder Weins:
'Weh, nun geht's schief!
Verfall! Verfall! Nie sank die Welt so tief!
Rom sank zur Hure und zur Huren-Bude,
Roms Cäsar sank zum Vieh, Gott selbst – ward Jude!'

Beim Anblick eines Schlafrocks

Kam, trotz schlumpichtem Gewande,
Einst der Deutsche zu Verstande,
Weh, wie hat sich das gewandt!
Eingeknöpft in strenge Kleider,
Überließ er seinem Schneider,
Seinem Bismarck – den Verstand!

An Spinoza

Dem 'Eins in Allem' liebend zugewandt,
Amore dei, selig aus Verstand –
Die Schuhe aus! welch dreimal heilig Land! –
– Doch unter dieser Liebe fraß
Ein heimlich glimmender Rachebrand,
Am Judengott fraß Judenhaß . . .
Einsiedler! Hab ich dich erkannt?

Once, I believe, in the year of the holy one

Once, I believe, in the year of the holy one
Spoke the Sibyll, drunk on wine,
'Woe, now, it goes crooked! Fall! Fall!
The world never sank so deep!
Rome sank to the whore and whorehouse,
Caesar became a beast and God himself – a Jew!'

The spectacle of the dressing gown

In spite of the scruffy gown, there
Was once a German understanding,
Woe, how that has changed!
Buttoned in a strange frock,
It surrendered to his tailor,
To his Bismarck – its understanding!

For Spinoza

The blessed understanding, lovingly
Dedicated to 'Each in All', *Amor dei* –
Off with the shoes! Three times Holy Land! –
Already a homely burning revenge
Gnaws under this love.
Jewish hate eats the Jewish God . . .
Hermit! Did I recognize you?

An die Jünger Darwins

Dieser braven Engeländer
Mittelmäßige Verständer
Nehmt ihr als 'Philosophie'?
Darwin neben Goethe setzen
Heißt: die *Majestät verletzen* –
Majestatem genii!

Heil euch, brave Karrenschieber

Heil euch, brave Karrenschieber,
Stets 'je länger, desto lieber',
Steifer stets an Kopf und Knie,
Unbegeistert, ungespäßig,
Unverwüstlich-mittelmäßig,
Sans genie et sans esprit!

Arthur Schopenhauer

Was er lehrte, ist abgetan;
Was er lebte, wird bleiben stahn:
Seht ihn nur an –
Niemandem war er untertan!

For Darwin's disciples

Do these brave Englishmen,
These mediocre intellects,
Name you as 'Philosophy'?
Set Darwin besides Goethe,
And call out: *Injured majesty –*
Majestic genius!

Hail to you, brave cart pushers

Hail to you, brave cart pushers
Always 'the longer, the better',
Standing stiff head to knee[5]
Unspirited, unfunny,
Indestructibly-mediocre
Sans genie et sans esprit!

Arthur Schopenhauer

What he taught, is settled;
How he lived, will stand:
Look at him –
He is subject to no one!

An Richard Wagner

Der du an jeder Fessel krankst,
Friedloser, unbefreiter Geist,
Siegreicher stets und doch gebundener,
Verekelt mehr und mehr, zerschundener,
Bis du aus jedem Balsam Gift dir trankst –,
Weh! Daß auch du am Kreuze niedersankst,
Auch du! Auch du – ein Überwundener!

Vor diesem Schauspiel steh ich lang,
Gefängnis atmend, Gram und Groll und Gruft,
Dazwischen Weihrauch-Wolken, Kirchen-Duft,
Mir fremd, mir schauerlich und bang.
Die Narrenkappe werf ich tanzend in die Luft,
Denn ich entsprang!

Wagner als Apostel der Keuschheit

– Ist das noch deutsch?
Aus deutschem Herzen kam dies schwüle Kreischen?
Und deutschen Leibs ist dies Sich-selbst-Zerfleischen?
Deutsch ist dies Priester-Hände-Spreizen,
Dies weihrauchdüftelnde Sinne-Reizen?
Und deutsch dies Stürzen, Stocken, Taumeln,
Dies zuckersüße Bimbambaumeln?
Dies Nonnen-Ängeln, Ave-Glockenbimmeln,
Dies ganze falsch verzückte Himmel-Überhimmeln? . . .

To Richard Wagner

You are hurt by every fetter,
Restless, *unfree* spirit,
Always triumphant and still bound, more and
More nauseated, destroyed, until you drink
The poison from every balm –
Woe! You too kneel at the cross,
You too! You too – Conqueror!

Always I stand before this spectacle,
Breathing prison, sorrow, resentment, and tomb,
Between consecrated clouds and church smells
Strange to me, sad and frightening to me.
I danced, throwing the fool's cap into the air,
Then I jumped away!

Wagner, the apostle of chastity

Is this still German?
From German hearts came these sultry shrieks?
And German bodies – this tearing of self to pieces?
German is this priestly-hand-shaking,
This consecrated tempting sensuousness?
And German is hurling, pausing, staggering,
This sugar sweet ding-dong dangling?
This nun ogling, Ave-bell ringing?
This whole false, rapturous heaven-over-heaven? . . .

Ist das noch deutsch?
Erwägt! Noch steht ihr an der Pforte . . .
Denn was ihr hört, ist Rom – *Roms Glaube ohne Worte*!

Is that still German?
Wake up! You are still standing at the gate . . .
What you can hear is Rome – *Rome's faith without words*!

'Scherz, List und Rache'
Vorspiel in deutschen Reimen (1882)

'Wit, Tricks and Revenge'
Prelude in German Rhymes (1882)

Einladung

Wagt's mit meiner Kost, ihr Esser!
Morgen schmeckt sie euch schon besser
Und schon übermorgen gut!
Wollt ihr dann noch mehr – so machen
Meine alten sieben Sachen
Mir zu sieben neuen Mut.

Mein Glück

Seit ich des Suchens müde ward,
Erlernte ich das Finden.
Seit mir ein Wind hielt Widerpart,
Segl' ich mit allen Winden.

Unverzagt

Wo du stehst, grab tief hinein!
Drunten ist die Quelle!
Laß die dunklen Männer schrein:
'Stets ist drunten – Hölle!'

Invitation

Taste my fare, you diners!
Tomorrow, it will taste even better
The day after tomorrow, it will be tastier still!
Do you want more – so give me
My seven old belongings
And my seven new courages.

My happiness

Since I was tired of searching
I learned to find.
Since a wind resisted me,
I sailed with all the winds.

Undaunted

Where you stand, dig deeply!
Dark is the source!
Let the dark men scream:
'Hell is always dark!'

Zwiegespräch

A. War ich krank? Bin ich genesen?
Und wer ist mein Arzt gewesen?
Wie vergaß ich alles das!
B. Jetzt erst glaub ich dich genesen:
Denn gesund ist, wer vergaß.

An die Tugendsamen

Unseren Tugenden auch sollen leicht dir Füße sich heben:
Gleich den Versen Homers müssen sie kommen *und gehn*!

Welt-Klugheit

Bleib nicht auf ebnem Feld!
Steig nicht zu hoch hinaus!
Am schönsten sieht die Welt
Von halber Höhe aus.

Vademecum-Vadetecum

Es lockt dich meine Art und Sprach,
Du folgest mir, du gehst mir nach?
Geh nur dir selber treulich nach: –
So folgst du mir – – gemach! gemach!

Dialogue

A. Was I ill? Did I get well?
And who was my Doctor?
I forgot it all!
B. I now believe that you have recovered:
Healthy is he who forgets.

For the virtuous

Our virtues shall lightly lift their feet:
Like Homer's verse, they must come, *and* go!

Worldly cleverness

Do not stand on an even field!
Do not climb up too high!
The world looks beautiful
From half its height!

Vademecum-Vadetecum

You are tempted by my speech and manner
You are following me, you go near me?
Go truly only to yourself –
So you will follow me – – Leisurely – leisurely!

Bei der dritten Häutung

Schon krümmt und bricht sich mir die Haut,
Schon giert mit neuem Drange,
So viel sie Erde schon verdaut,
Nach Erd in mir die Schlange.
Schon kriech ich zwischen Stein und Gras
Hungrig auf krummer Fährte,
Zu essen das, was stets ich aß,
Dich, Schlangenkost, dich, Erde!

Meine Rosen

Ja! Mein Glück – es will beglücken –
Alles Glück will ja beglücken!
Wollt ihr meine Rosen pflücken?

Müßt euch bücken und verstecken
Zwischen Fels und Dornenhecken,
Oft die Fingerchen euch lecken!

Denn mein Glück – es liebt das Necken!
Denn mein Glück – es liebt die Tücken! –
Wollt ihr meine Rosen pflücken?

Near the third skin

Already my skin curves and breaks,
Already my new desires exalt,
So much earth has been digested,
The earth is the snake in me.
Already I crawl between stone and grass
Hungry upon my crooked path,
To eat, what I always ate,
You, the snake's fare, you, the earth.

My roses

Yes! My happiness – it will bring –
All happiness will it bring!
Would you like to pick my roses?

You must bend down and hide
Between the rock and thorny hedges,
And often, lick your little fingers!

Because my happiness loves to tease!
Because my happiness loves malice!
Would you like to pick my roses?

Der Verächter

Vieles laß ich falln und rollen,
Und ihr nennt mich drum Verächter.
Wer da trinkt aus allzuvollen
Bechern, läßt viel falln und rollen –,
Denkt vom Weine drum nicht schlechter.

Das Sprichwort spricht.

Scharf und milde, grob und fein,
Vertraut und seltsam, schmutzig und rein,
Der Narren und Weisen Stelldichein:
Dies alles bin ich, will ich sein,
Taube zugleich, Schlange und Schwein!

An einen Lichtfreund

Willst du nicht Aug und Sinn ermatten,
Lauf auch der Sonne nach im Schatten!

Für Tänzer

Glattes Eis
Ein Paradeis
Für den, der gut zu tanzen weiß.

The contemptible

I let many things fall and roll around
And you call me contemptuous.
Who drinks from overflowing mugs
Lets many things fall and roll –,
But I do not think badly of the wine.

The word speaker speaks

Sharp and mild, coarse and fine,
Confident and strange, dirty and pure
The fool and the wise speak:
This is all I am, and will be,
Like a pigeon, snake, and swine.

For a bright friend

Will you not shade your eyes and mind?
Then you can run after the sun in the shade!

For the dancers

Smooth ice
A paradise
For those who dance well.

Der Brave

Lieber aus ganzem Holz eine Feindschaft
Als eine geleimte Freundschaft!

Rost

Auch Rost tut not: Scharfsein ist nicht genung!
Sonst sagt man stets von dir: 'er ist zu jung!'

Aufwärts

'Wie komm ich am besten den Berg hinan?' –
Steig nur hinauf und denk nicht dran!

Spruch des Gewaltmenschen

Bitte nie! Laß dies Gewimmer!
Nimm, ich bitte dich, nimm immer!

Schmale Seelen

Schmale Seelen sind mir verhaßt:
Da steht nichts Gutes, nichts Böses fast.

The brave one

Better to have a wooden hostility
Than a glutinous friendship!

Rust

Rust has its needs, sharpness is not enough
Otherwise one will always say of you – ‘He is too young!’

Upwards

‘How can I best climb the mountain?’
Climb up! And do not think about it!

The speech of the powerful

Please never! Stop your whimpering!
Take, I beg you, always take!

Narrow souls

I hate narrow souls:
Their almost neither good nor bad.

Der unfreiwillige Verführer

Er schoß ein leeres Wort zum Zeitvertreib
Ins Blaue – und doch fiel darob ein Weib.

Zur Erwägung

Zwiefacher Schmerz ist leichter zu tragen
Als *ein* Schmerz: willst du darauf es wagen?

Gegen die Hoffart

Blas dich nicht auf: sonst bringet dich
Zum Platzen schon ein kleiner Stich.

Mann und Weib

'Raub dir das Weib, für das dein Herze fühlt!' –
So denkt der Mann; das Weib raubt nicht, es stiehlt.

The unwilling seducer

He casts an empty word to wile away the time:
Into the blue – and yet a woman fell for it.

Consideration

Double pain is easier to bear
Than only one pain: Would you dare it?

Against arrogance

Do not blow yourself up: otherwise only
A small stab will make you burst.

Man and woman

‘Rob the woman for whom your heart beats!’ –
So thinks the man; the woman does not rob, she steals.

Interpretation

Leg ich mich aus, so leg ich mich hinein:
Ich kann nicht selbst mein Interprete sein.
Doch wer nur steigt auf seiner eignen Bahn,
Trägt auch mein Bild zu hellerm Licht hinan.

Pessimisten-Arznei

Du klagst, daß nichts dir schmackhaft sei?
Noch immer, Freund, die alten Mucken?
Ich hör dich lästern, lärmen, spucken –
Geduld und Herz bricht mir dabei.
Folg mir, mein Freund! Entschließ dich frei,
Ein fettes Krötchen zu verschlucken,
Geschwind und ohne hinzugucken! –
Das hilft dir von der Dyspepsei!

Interpretation

I lie away from myself as I lie in myself:
I cannot be my own interpreter.
He who already climbs on his own path,
Will carry my image into bright light.

Pessimistic medical advice

You complain you have no taste?
Still always the old snag, my friend?
I can hear you moan, groaning and spit –
It breaks my heart and patience.
Follow me, my friend, decide freely,
Swallow a little fat toad
Quickly and without looking! –
It will help your Dyspepsia!

Bitte

Ich kenne mancher Menschen Sinn
Und weiß nicht, wer ich selber bin!
Mein Auge ist mir viel zu nah –
Ich bin nicht, was ich seh und sah.
Ich wollte mir schon besser nützen,
Könnt ich mir selber ferner sitzen.
Zwar nicht so ferne wie mein Feind!
Zu fern sitzt schon der nächste Freund –
Doch zwischen dem und mir die Mitte!
Erratet ihr, um was ich bitte?

Meine Härte

Ich muß weg über hundert Stufen,
Ich muß empor und hör euch rufen:
'Hart bist du! Sind wir denn von Stein?' –
Ich muß weg über hundert Stufen,
Und niemand möchte Stufe sein.

Der Wandrer

'Kein Pfad mehr! Abgrund rings und Totenstille!' –
So wolltest du's! Vom Pfade wich dein Wille!
Nun, Wandrer, gilt's! Nun blicke kalt und klar!
Verloren bist du, glaubst du – an Gefahr.

Request

I know many men's minds
And do not know what I am!
My eye is much too close to me –
I am not what I see and saw.
It would be more useful for me if
I could sit further away from myself.
Indeed, not so far away as my enemy!
My next friend already sits too far away –
Already between him and me – the middle!
Can you guess what I request?

My cruelty

I must go over a hundred steps,
I must go upwards and hear you cry:
'You are cruel! Are we made of stone?' –
I must go over a hundred steps,
And nobody wants to be a step.

The wanderer

'No path any more! Only abyss and deathly silence!' –
You wanted this! From the path your will has strayed!
Now, wanderer, it was worth it! Now, look cold and clear!
You are lost, you believe – in danger.

Trost für Anfänger

Seht das Kind umgrunzt von Schweinen,
Hilflos, mit verkrümmten Zehn!
Weinen kann es, nichts als weinen –
Lernt es jemals stehn und gehn?
Unverzagt! Bald, sollt ich meinen,
Könnt das Kind ihr tanzen sehn!
Steht es erst auf beiden Beinen,
Wird's auch auf dem Kopfe stehn.

Sternen-Egoismus

Rollt ich mich rundes Rollefaß
Nicht um mich selbst ohn Unterlaß,
Wie hielt ich's aus, ohne anzubrennen,
Der heißen Sonne nachzurennen?

Der Nächste

Nah hab den Nächsten ich nicht gerne:
Fort mit ihm in die Höh und Ferne!
Wie würd er sonst zu meinem Sterne? –

Consolation for beginners

See the child surrounded by pigs,
Helpless, and with crooked toes!
It can cry and do nothing else –
Will it ever learn to stand and walk?
Immediately!
I see that the child can dance!
First it stands upon both legs,
It will soon stand on its head.

Egoism of stars

I roll myself around in a barrel, though
I do not roll myself around without limits,
How can I bear it without getting burnt?
Running toward the scorching sun?

The next one

I do not like the next one near to me:
Away with him into the high and far!
How else could he become my star?

Der verkappte Heilige

Daß dein Glück uns nicht bedrücke,
Legst du um dich Teufelstücke,
Teufelswitz und Teufelskleid.
Doch umsonst! Aus deinem Blicke
Blickt hervor die Heiligkeit!

Der Unfreie

A. Er steht und horcht: was konnt ihn irren?
Was hört er vor den Ohren schwirren?
Was war's, das ihn darniederschlug?
B. Wie jeder, der einst Ketten trug,
Hort überall er – Kettenklirren.

Disguised holiness

Your happiness must not oppress us,
Cover yourself with the Devil's piece,
Devil's wit and the devil's gown.
But, in vain! From your
Gaze shows holiness!

The involuntary

A. He stands and listens: What can be wrong?
What can he hear with buzzing ears?
What was it that beat him down?
B. Like everyone who once wore chains,
He can hear over everything else – rattling chains.

Der Einsame

Verhaßt ist mir das Folgen und das Führen.
Gehorchen? Nein! Und aber nein – Regieren!
Wer *sich* nicht schrecklich ist, macht niemand Schrecken.
Und nur wer Schrecken macht, kann andre führen.
Verhaßt ist mir's schon, selber mich zu führen!
Ich liebe es, gleich Wald- und Meerestieren,
Mich für ein gutes Weilchen ru verlieren,
In holder Irrnis grüblerisch zu hocken
Von ferne her mich endlich heimzulocken,
Mich selber zu mir selber zu verführen.

Seneca et hoc genus omne

Das schreibt und schreibt sein unausstehlich
Weises Larifari,
Als gält es *primum scribere*,
Deinde philosophari.

Eis

Ja! Mitunter mach ich Eis:
Nützlich ist Eis zum Verdauen!
Hättet ihr viel zu verdauen,
O wie liebtet ihr mein Eis!

The lonely one

I hate the follower and the leader.
To be followed! No! And not to Rule!
Who himself is not frightening, give no one a fright.
And only he who frightens can lead others.
I hate being led by myself!
I love to lose myself for a little while,
Like the forest and sea creatures,
To squat broodingly in charming error,
From far away, I finally wish to lure myself home,
Myself to myself, to be led astray.

Seneca et hoc genus omne

One writes and writes to stand outside –
The wise Larifari[6] exposes,
As if to say: *primum scribere*
Deinde philosophari.[7]

Ice

Yes! Occasionally I make ice:
Ice is good for the digestion!
If you have a lot to digest,
Oh, how you will love my ice!

Jugendschriften

Meiner Weisheit A und O
Klang mir hier: was hört ich doch!
Jetzo klingt mir's nicht mehr so,
Nur das ewge Ah! und Oh!
Meiner Jugend hör ich noch.

Vorsicht

In jener Gegend reist man jetzt nicht gut;
Und hast du Geist, sei doppelt auf der Hut!
Man lockt und liebt dich, bis man dich zerreißt:
Schwarmgeister sind's –: da fehlt es stets an Geist!

Der Fromme spricht

Gott liebt uns, *weil* er uns erschuf! –
'Der Mensch schuf Gott!' – sagt drauf ihr Feinen.
Und soll nicht lieben, was er schuf?
Soll's gar, *weil* er es schuf, verneinen?
Das hinkt, das trägt des Teufels Huf.

Youthful writing

My wisdom A and O
Here it sounds: I already hear it!
It does not sound like that anymore,
Only the everlasting Ah! and Oh!
I can still hear my youth.

Caution

One does not like to travel in that district;
And if you have spirit, be doubly careful!
One tempts and loves you, until you are torn apart:
They are ghostly spirits – only the spirit is missing!

The pious one speaks

God loves us, because he created us! –
‘Man created God!’ – so say the educated.
Shall he not love what he created?
Shall he denounce what he created?
He limps, and wears the devil’s hoof.

Im Sommer

Im Schweiße unsres Angesichts
Solln unser Brot wir essen?
Im Schweiße ißt man lieber nichts,
Nach weiser Ärzte Ermessen.
Der Hundsstern winkt: woran gebricht's?
Was will sein feurig Winken?
Im Schweiße unsres Angesichts
Solln unsren Wein wir trinken!

Ohne Neid

Ja, neidlos blickt er: und ihr ehrt ihn drum?
Er blickt sich nicht nach euren Ehren um;
Er hat des Adlers Auge für die Ferne,
Er sieht euch nicht! – er sieht nur Sterne, Sterne!

In the summer

Considering how we are sweating
Shall we eat our bread?
One should not eat in the heat,
According to the good Doctor's advice.
The Dog Star[8] winks: where did it break?
What will its fiery wink do?
Considering how we are sweating
We shall drink our wine!

Without envy

Yes, he stares without envy: and you honor him for that?
He does not look around for your honors;
He has the eagle's eye for the distance,
He does not see you! – he sees only stars, stars!

Heraklitismus

Alles Glück auf Erden,
Freunde, gibt der Kampf!
Ja, um Freund zu werden,
Braucht es Pulverdampf!
Eins in Drein sind Freunde:
Brüder vor der Not,
Gleiche vor dein Feinde,
Freie – – vor dem Tod!

Grundsatz der Allzufeinen

Lieber auf den Zehen noch
Als auf allen vieren!
Lieber durch ein Schlüsselloch
Als durch offne Türen!

Zuspruch

Auf Ruhm hast du den Sinn gericht?
Dann acht der Lehre:
Beizeiten leiste frei Verzicht
Auf Ehre!

Heraklitismus

All luck upon the earth,
My friend, is given in battle!
Yes, to become a friend,
One needs steam and powder!
One in three friends are:
Brothers in need
Equal before the enemy
Free – before death!

Ground rules for snobs

Better to stand on your toes
Than on all fours!
Better to go through a keyhole
Than through open doors!

Encouragement

Your mind aims for glory?
Then take note of the way:
At all times, be free to
Deny with honor!

Der Gründliche

Ein Forscher ich? O spart dies Wort! –
Ich bin nur *schwer* – so manche Pfund!
Ich falle, falle immerfort
Und endlich auf den Grund!

Für immer

'Heut komm ich, weil mir's heute frommt' –
Denkt jeder, der für immer kommt.
Was ficht ihn an der Welt Gered:
'Du kommst zu früh! Du kommst zu spät!'

Urteile der Müden

Der Sonne fluchen alle Matten;
Der Bäume Wert ist ihnen – Schatten!

Niedergang

'Er sinkt, er fallt jetzt' – höhnt ihr hin und wieder;
Die Wahrheit ist: er steigt zu euch hernieder!
Sein Überglück ward ihm zum Ungemach,
Sein Überlicht geht eurem Dunkel nach.

The founder

Me, an explorer? Oh, please spare the word! –
I am only *heavy* – so many pounds!
I am falling, always falling
And finally upon the ground!

Forever

'Today I come, because I feel good today' –
So thinks everybody who comes for good.
Worldly gossip bothers him:
You come too early! You come too late!

Verdict of the weary

The sun condemns all the weary;
The worth of a tree is its – shadow!

Decline

'He sinks, he falls!' I hear you here and there.
The truth is: he climbs *down* to you!
His joy becomes his undoing,
His bright light approaches your darkness.

Gegen die Gesetze

Von heut an hängt an härner Schnur
Um meinen Hals die Stunden-Uhr;
Von heut an hört der Sterne Lauf,
Sonn, Hahnenschrei und Schatten auf,
Und was mir je die Zeit verkündt,
Das ist jetzt stumm und taub und blind: –
Es schweigt mir jegliche Natur
Beim Ticktack von Gesetz und Uhr.

Der Weise spricht

Dem Volke fremd und nützlich doch dein Volke,
Zieh ich des Weges, Sonne bald, bald Wolke –
Und immer über diesem Volke!

Den Kopf verloren

Sie hat jetzt Geist – wie kam's, daß sie ihn fand?
Ein Mann verlor durch sie jüngst den Verstand.
Sein Kopf war reich vor diesem Zeitvertreibe:
Zum Teufel ging sein Kopf – nein! nein! zum Weibe!

Against the law

From today onwards, on a tight cord
Around my neck will hang an hour-clock;
The star's course spoke today
Upon the sun, the cock's crow
Upon the shadows, and what
Time always tells me is now
Deaf, dumb and blind: Nature is silent
For me with the tick-tock of law and clock.

The wise one speaks

I am a stranger to the people but useful to the people,
I go on my way, close to sun, close to cloud –
And always over the people!

To lose one's head

She has spirit – how did she find it?
A man lost his sense through her.
His head was ruled by anxiety:
To the devil went his head – No! No! – to a woman!

Fromme Wünsche

'Mögen alle Schlüssel doch
Flugs verlorengehen,
Und in jedem Schlüsselloch
Sich der Dietrich drehen!'
Also denkt zu jeder Frist
Jeder, der – ein Dietrich ist.

Mit dem Fuße schreiben

Ich schreib nicht mit der Hand allein:
Der Fuß will stets mit Schreiber sein.
Fest, frei und tapfer läuft er mir
Bald durch das Feld, bald durchs Papier.

'Menschliches, Allzumenschliches'. Ein Buch

Schwermütig scheu, solang du rückwärts schaust,
Der Zukunft trauend, wo du selbst dir traust:
O Vogel, rechn' ich dich den Adlern zu?
Bist du Minervas Liebling U-hu-hu?

Best wishes

'May all keys
Quickly disappear
And through each keyhole
A skeleton key will turn!'
Also, think, in all times,
Of everyone – who is a skeleton key.

To write with one's feet

I write not with my hand alone:
The foot shall be my pen.
Festive, free and brave it runs,
Sometimes through the field, sometimes through the paper.

Human, all too human: *a book*

You look back sadly for so long,
Trusting the future, where you trust yourself:
Oh, bird, will I trust you,
Are you Minerva's darling U-hu-hu?

Meinem Leser

Ein gut Gebiß und einen guten Magen –
Dies wünsch ich dir!
Und hast du erst mein Buch vertragen,
Verträgst du dich gewiß mit mir!

Der realistische Maler

'Treu die Natur und ganz!' – Wie fängt er's an:
Wann wäre je Natur im Bilde *abgetan*?
Unendlich ist das kleinste Stück der Welt! –
Er malt zuletzt davon, was ihm *gefällt*.
Und was gefällt ihm? Was er malen *kann*!

Dichter-Eitelkeit

Gebt mir Leim nur: denn zum Leime
Find ich selber mir schon Holz!
Sinn in vier unsinnge Reime
Legen – ist kein kleiner Stolz!

For my readers

Good teeth, a good stomach –
That's what I wish you!
And when you have first digested my book
You will surely agree with me!

The realistic painter

'Trust nature completely!' How does he start?
Since when was nature shown on a canvas?
Untimely is the smallest corner of the world! –
He paints what he *likes*.
And what does he like? What he *can* paint!

The poet's vanity

Only give me glue:
I can find the wood myself!
Sense in four nonsensical rhymes
Is not a small object of pride!

Wählerischer Geschmack

Wenn man frei mich wählen ließe,
Wählt ich gern ein Plätzchen mir
Mitten drin im Paradiese:
Gerner noch – vor seiner Tür!

Die krumme Nase

Die Nase schauet trutziglich
Ins Land, der Nüster blähet sich –
Drum fällst du, Nashorn ohne Horn,
Mein stolzes Menschlein, stets sich vorn!
Und stets beisammen findt sich das:
Gerader Stolz, gekrümmte Nas.

Die Feder kritzelt

Die Feder kritzelt: Hölle das!
Bin ich verdammt zum Kritzeln-Müssen? –
So greif ich kühn zum Tintenfaß
Und schreib mit dicken Tintenflüssen.
Wie läuft das hin, so voll, so breit!
Wie glückt mir alles, wie ich's treibe!
Zwar fehlt der Schrill die Deutlichkeit –
Was tut's? Wer liest denn, was ich schreibe?

Chosen enjoyment

If I could choose freely,
I would gladly choose a little place
In the middle of Paradise:
Better still – in front of its door!

The crooked nose

The nose shows itself defiantly
In the land and blows its nostrils –
There you fell, Rhinoceros, without a horn,
My proud little being, always in front!
And always there it will be:
Upright pride, crooked nose.

The pen scribbles

The pen scribbles: to hell with that!
Am I condemned to scribbling?
Boldly I reach for the inkwell
And write in thick inky floods.
It runs away, so full and broad!
How happy I am, as I do it!
The writing is not very clear –
What does it matter? Who reads what I write?

Höhere Menschen

Der steigt empor – ihn soll man loben!
Doch jener kommt allzeit von oben!
Der lebt dem Lobe selbst enthoben,
Der *ist* von droben!

Der Skeptiker spricht

Halb ist dein Leben um,
Der Zeiger rückt, die Seele schaudert dir!
Lang schweift sie schon herum
Und sucht, und fand nicht – und sie zaudert hier?

Halb ist dein Leben um:
Schmerz war's und Irrtum, Stund um Stund dahier!
Was suchst du noch? *Warum*? – –
Dies eben such ich – Grund um Grund dafür!

Higher men

He climbs up – you must praise him!
But this one comes from above!
He is relieved of praise,
He is from above!

The skeptic speaks

Your life is half way around,
Time moves on, your soul shudders!
She hovers long already, she sought
But did not find – and she hesitates here?

Your life is half way through:
It was pain and error, hour after hour!
What are you still looking for?
And why? – I am looking for reason after reason!

Ecce homo

Ja! Ich weiß, woher ich stamme!
Ungesättigt gleich der Flamme
Glühe und verzehr ich mich.
Licht wird alles, was ich fasse,
Kohle alles, was ich lasse:
Flamme bin ich sicherlich.

Sternen-Moral

Vorausbestimmt zur Sternenbahn,
Was geht dich. Stern, das Dunkel an?

Roll selig hin durch diese Zeit
Ihr Elend sei dir fremd und weit!

Der fernsten Welt gehört dein Schein:
Mitleid soll Sünde für dich sein!

Nur *ein* Gebot gilt dir: sei rein!

Ecce homo

Yes! I know where I come from!
Like an insatiable flame,
I glow and devour myself.
Everything I hold becomes bright
What I leave is like coal:
I am flame.

Morality of stars

Destined on the way of stars,
Do you not care about darkness, Star?

You roll divinely through time!
Their misery is strange and far way from you!

Your shine belongs to far away worlds:
Pity is sin for you!

Only *one* rule for you: be pure!

Lieder des Prinzen Vogelfrei
(1887)

Songs of Prince Vogelfrei (1887)

An Goethe

Das Unvergängliche
Ist nur dein Gleichnis!
Gott, der Verfängliche,
Ist Dichter-Erschleichnis . . .

Welt-Rad, das rollende,
Streift Ziel auf Ziel:
Not – nennt's der Grollende,
Der Narr nennt's – Spiel . . .

Welt-Spiel, das herrische
Mischt Sein und Schein: –
Das Ewig-Närrische
Mischt *uns* – hinein! . . .

Dichters Berufung

Als ich jüngst, mich zu erquicken,
Unter dunklen Bäumen saß,
Hört ich ticken, leise ticken,
Zierlich, wie nach Takt und Maß.
Böse wurd ich, zog Gesichter, –
Endlich aber gab ich nach,
Bis ich gar, gleich einem Dichter,
Selber mit im Ticktack sprach.

For Goethe

Tenuousness –
Is your only equality!
God the artist
Is a poet's pretension . . .

The wheel of the world rolls
And strikes target after target:
Suffering, the grumbler calls it.
The fool calls it – a game . . .

The mighty world game
Mixes being and illusion: –
Eternal foolishness
Mixes *us* – into it! . . .

The poet's profession

In my youth, as I sat under
A shady tree to refresh myself,
I heard a quiet tick, ticking,
Dainty, gentle and measured.
I became cross and pulled faces, –
Finally however I gave in,
Until I spoke, like a poet,
With the tick tock myself.

Wie mir so im Verse-Machen
Silb um Silb ihr Hopsa sprang,
Mußt ich plötzlich lachen, lachen
Eine Viertelstunde lang.
Du ein Dichter? Du ein Dichter?
Steht's mit deinem Kopf so schlecht?
– 'Ja, mein Herr, Sie sind ein Dichter'
Achselzuckt der Vogel Specht.

Wessen harr ich hier im Busche?
Wem doch laur' ich Räuber auf?
Ist's ein Spruch? Ein Bild? Im Husche
Sitzt mein Reim ihm hintendrauf.
Was nur schlüpft und hüpft, gleich sticht der
Dichter sich's zum Vers zurecht.
– 'Ja, mein Herr, Sie sind ein Dichter'
Achselzuckt der Vogel Specht.

Reime, mein ich, sind wie Pfeile?
Wie das zappelt, zittert, springt,
Wenn der Pfeil in edle Teile
Des Lazerten-Leibchens dringt!
Ach, ihr sterbt dran, arme Wichter,
Oder taumelt wie bezecht!
– 'Ja, mein Herr, Sie sind ein Dichter'
Achselzuckt der Vogel Specht.

And so when I wrote, as syllable
After syllable hopped up in me,
I suddenly had to laugh, laugh
For a quarter of an hour.
You a poet? You a poet?
Are you right in the head?
– 'Yes sir, you are a poet'
Shrugged the woodpecker.

Why do I linger in these bushes?
Why do I wait for robbers?
Is it a poem? Or, a picture? Scurrying away,
My rhyme slips into the background.
What only slips, hops and stings like a
Poet who turns back to his verse.
– 'Yes sir, you are a poet'
Shrugged the woodpecker.

Rhymes, I mean, are like arrows?
The arrow struggles, shivers, jumps
And penetrates the noble part
Of the lovely stomach.
Alas, you will die, poor creatures,
Or stagger as you are stung!
– 'Yes sir, you are a poet!'
Shrugged the woodpecker.

Schiefe Sprüchlein voller Eile,
Trunkne Wörtlein, wie sich's drängt!
Bis ihr alle, Zeil an Zeile,
An der Ticktack-Kette hängt.
Und es gibt grausam Gelichter,
Das dies – – freut? Sind Dichter – – schlecht?
– 'Ja, mein Herr, Sie sind ein Dichter'
Achselzuckt der Vogel Specht.

Höhnst du, Vogel? Willst du scherzen?
Steht's mit meinem Kopf schon schlimm,
Schlimmer stünd's mit meinem Herzen?
Fürchte, fürchte meinen Grimm! –
Doch der Dichter – Reime flicht er
Selbst im Grimm noch schlecht und recht.
– 'Ja, mein Herr, Sie sind ein Dichter'
Achselzuckt der Vogel Specht.

Im Süden

So häng ich denn auf krummem Aste
Und schaukle meine Müdigkeit.
Ein Vogel lud mich her zu Gaste,
Ein Vogelnest ist's, drin ich raste.
Wo hin ich doch? Ach, weit! Ach, weit!

Crooked words, full of haste,
Drunken words, urge me on!
Until they all, row after row,
Hang on tick tock chains and
Provoke gruesome laughter.
Is this – amusing? Are poets – bad?
– 'Yes sir, you are a poet'
Shrugged the woodpecker.

Do you taunt me, bird? Do you joke?
Is my head already bad,
And worse still my heart?
Be afraid, afraid of my fury! –
Still the poet – twines his rhyme
In his fury, still bad and right.
– 'Yes sir, you are a poet!'
Shrugged the woodpecker.

In the south

I hang on a crooked branch,
And, my tiredness swings.
A bird invites me to be his guest,
A bird's nest is where I rest.
Where am I? Far way! Far away!

Das weiße Meer liegt eingeschlafen,
Und purpurn steht ein Segel drauf.
Fels, Feigenbäume, Turm und Hafen,
Idylle rings, Geblök von Schafen, –
Unschuld des Südens, nimm mich auf!

Nur Schritt für Schritt – das ist kein Leben,
Stets Bein vor Bein macht deutsch und schwer.
Ich hieß den Wind mich aufwärts heben,
Ich lernte mit den Vögeln schweben, –
Nach Süden flog ich übers Meer.

Vernunft! Verdrießliches Geschäfte!
Das bringt uns allzubald ans Ziel!
Im Fliegen lernt ich, was mich äffte, –
Schon fühl ich Mut und Blut und Säfte
Zu neuem Leben, neuem Spiel . . .

Einsam zu denken nenn ich weise,
Doch einsam singen – wäre dumm!
So hört ein Lied zu eurem Preise
Und setzt euch still um mich im Kreise,
Ihr schlimmen Vögelchen, herum!

The white sea sleeps and a sail
Stands upon a purple surface,
Rocks, fig trees, tower and harbor,
Idyll all around, the bleating of sheep, –
Innocence of the South, take me!

Only step by step – that is not life,
Leg to leg makes German and heavy.
I called the wind to lift me up,
I learned to fly with the birds –
I fly to the south over the sea.

Reason! Annoying business!
It will bring us to our goal!
In flight, I learned what made me silly, –
Already I feel courage, blood and sap
For new life, a new game . . .

To think alone is wise,
But to sing alone is dumb!
Listen to a song of praise and
Sit in a circle around me,
You bad little birds!

So jung, so falsch, so umgetrieben –
Scheint ganz ihr mir gemacht zum Lieben
Und jedem schönen Zeitvertreib?
Im Norden – ich gesteh's mit Zaudern –
Liebt ich ein Weibchen, alt zum Schaudern:
'Die Wahrheit' hieß dies alte Weib . . .

Die fromme Beppa

Solang noch hübsch mein Leibchen,
Lohnt sich's schon, fromm zu sein.
Man weiß, Gott liebt die Weibchen,
Die hübschen obendrein.
Er wird's dem armen Mönchlein
Gewißlich gern verzeihn,
Daß er, gleich manchem Mönchlein,
So gern will bei mir sein.

Kein grauer Kirchenvater!
Nein, jung noch und oft rot,
Oft trotz dein grausten Kater
Voll Eifersucht und Not.
Ich liebe nicht die Greise,
Er liebt die Alten nicht:
Wie wunderlich und weise
Hat Gott dies eingericht!

So young, false, unruly –
It seems you were meant to love me
And wile away the time with me?
To the North – I confess with a shudder –
I love a woman, who is used to shivering:
'The truth' was called this old woman . . .

The pious Beppa

As long as you are still pretty,
It's worth it to be good and pious.
One knows, God loves young women,
Especially the pretty ones.
It is the poor monks that
He will surely pardon,
Who, like the many monks,
Wish to be with me.

Not a grey pastor!
No, still young and blushing,
I often trot like a grey tomcat
Full of enthusiasm and piety.
I do not love the old man,
He does not love the old:
How wondrous and wise
Has God arranged all this!

Die Kirche weiß zu leben,
Sie prüft Herz und Gesicht.
Stets will sie mir vergeben, –
Ja, wer vergibt mir nicht!
Man lispelt mit dem Mündchen,
Man knixt und geht hinaus,
Und mit dem neuen Sündchen
Löscht man das alte aus.

Gelobt sei Gott auf Erden,
Der hübsche Mädchen liebt
Und derlei Herzbeschwerden
Sich selber gern vergibt.
Solang noch hübsch mein Leibchen,
Lohnt sich's schon fromm zu sein:
Als altes Wackelweibchen
Mag mich der Teufel frein!

Der geheimnisvolle Nachen

Gestern nachts, als alles schlief,
Kaum der Wind mit ungewissen
Seufzern durch die Gassen lief,
Gab mir Ruhe nicht das Kissen,
Noch der Mohn, noch, was sonst tief
Schlafen macht, – ein gut Gewissen.

The church knows how to live,
She examines heart and opinion.
She always forgives me, –
Yes, who does not forgive me!
I lisp with my mouth
I genuflect and depart
And with my new sins,
I extinguish the old ones.

Praise be God upon the earth,
Who loves pretty girls
Who occupies hearts
And willingly forgives himself.
As long as you are still pretty,
It's worth it, to be good and pious:
Since I am an old tattering woman,
The devil may court me!

The mysterious boat

Last night, as everything slept,
The wind sighed with unknowing,
Running through the lane,
I found no rest upon my pillow
It is the moon, still, that gives me
A deep sleep, – a good conscience.

Endlich schlug ich mir den Schlaf
Aus dem Sinn und lief zum Strande.
Mondhell war's und mild, ich traf
Mann und Kahn auf warmem Sande,
Schläfrig beide, Hirt und Schaf: –
Schläfrig stieß der Kahn vom Lande.

Eine Stunde, leicht auch zwei,
Oder war's ein Jahr? – da sanken
Plötzlich mir Sinn und Gedanken
In ein ewiges Einerlei,
Und ein Abgrund ohne Schranken
Tat sich auf: – da war's vorbei!

– Morgen kam: auf schwarzen Tiefen
steht ein Kahn und ruht und ruht . . .
Was geschah? so rief's, so riefen
Hundert bald: was gab es? Blut? – –
Nichts geschah! Wir schliefen, schliefen
Alle – ach, so gut! so gut!

Liebeserklärung

bei der aber der Dichter in eine Grube fiel

O Wunder! Fliegt er noch?
Er steigt empor, und seine Flügel ruhn?
Was hebt und trägt ihn doch?
Was ist ihm Ziel und Zug und Zügel nun?

I brushed sleep away from my
Senses and ran to the beach.
Moonlight shone and I met man and boat
Calmly upon the warm sands,
Sleepy both – shepherd and sheep –
Sleepy the boat slips away from land.

One hour, maybe two,
Or, was it a year? – to me
Suddenly sense and thought
Seem to be an eternal sameness,
Amid this abyss without limits,
I *do* myself upon the past.

– Morning came, a boat stands
In the black depth and rests – rests . . .
What happened? She called – hundreds
Called me: what was it? Blood? – –
Nothing happened? We sleep, sleep
All sleeps – ah, so good! So good!

A proposal of love

when unfortunately the poet fell into a pit

Oh, Wonder! He still flies?
He rises up, his wings are resting?
What lifts and carries him?
What is now his target, pull, and power?

  Gleich Stern und Ewigkeit
Lebt er in Höhn jetzt, die das Leben flieht,
  Mitleidig selbst dem Neid –:
Und hoch flog, wer ihn auch nur schweben sieht!

  O Vogel Albatros!
Zur Höhe treibt's mit ewgem Triebe mich.
  Ich dachte dein: da floß
Mir Trän um Träne, – ja, ich liebe dich!

Lied eines theokritischen Ziegenhirten

Da lieg ich, krank im Gedärm, –
Mich fressen die Wanzen.
Und drüben noch Licht und Lärm!
Ich hör's, sie tanzen . . .

Sie wollte um diese Stund
Zu mir sich schleichen.
Ich warte wie ein Hund, –
Es kommt kein Zeichen.

Das Kreuz, als sie's versprach?
Wie konnte sie lügen?
– Oder läuft sie jedem nach,
Wie meine Ziegen?

Like stars and eternity
He now lives in heights, fleeing life,
Compassionate even to jealousy . . .
Flying high, you see only in suspense!

Oh, Albatross bird,
Impulse makes me fly high,
I thought of you:
My tears flow, – yes, I love you!

Song of a theocritical goatherd

I lie down, sick in my guts –
Bugs are eating me.
And still – light and noise!
I can hear them – dancing . . .

They creep around me
At every hour.
I wait like a dog, –
No sign comes.

Is it of the cross that you speak?
How could you lie?
– Or, do you run after everyone,
To my goats?

Woher ihr seidner Rock? –
Ah, meine Stolze?
Es wohnt noch mancher Bock
An diesem Holze?

– Wie kraus und giftig macht
Verliebtes Warten!
So wächst bei schwüler Nacht
Giftpilz im Garten.

Die Liebe zehrt an mir
Gleich sieben Übeln, –
Nichts mag ich essen schier.
Lebt wohl, ihr Zwiebeln!

Der Mond ging schon ins Meer,
Müd sind alle Sterne,
Grau kommt der Tag daher, –
Ich stürbe gerne.

'Diesen ungewissen Seelen'

Diesen ungewissen Seelen
Bin ich grimmig gram.
All ihr Ehren ist ein Quälen,
All ihr Lob ist Selbstverdruß und Scham.

Into her silken skirt? –
Oh, my proud one?
This forest wants
Many bucks?

– Waiting for love makes
Me cross and poisonous!
In the sultry night, poisonous
Mushrooms grow in my garden.

Love consumes me
Like seven challenges –
I will not eat that which is close.
Live well, you onions!

The moon goes into the sea,
The stars are tired,
The day dawns grey, –
I willingly die.

'These uncertain souls'

I am severely grieved by
These uncertain souls
All their honor is in vain.
All their praise is self-denial and shame.

Daß ich nicht an *ihrem* Stricke
Ziehe durch die Zeit,
Dafür grüßt mich ihrer Blicke
Giftig-süßer, hoffnungsloser Neid.

Möchten sie mir herzhaft fluchen
Und die Nase drehn!
Dieser Augen hilflos Suchen
Soll bei mir auf ewig irregehn.

Narr in Verzweiflung

Ach! Was ich schrieb auf Tisch und Wand
Mit Narrenherz und Narrenhand,
Das sollte Tisch und Wand mir zieren? . . .

Doch *ihr* sagt: 'Narrenhände schmieren, –
Und Tisch und Wand soll man purgieren,
Bis auch die letzte Spur verschwand!'

Erlaubt! Ich lege Hand mit an –,
Ich lernte Schwamm und Besen führen,
Als Kritiker, als Wassermann.

Doch, wenn die Arbeit abgetan,
Säh gern ich euch, ihr Überweisen,
Mit Weisheit Tisch und Wand besch . . .

I wander through time
Hung not by their ropes,
They greet me with their sweet
Toxic-sweet, hopeless envy.

They curse me wholeheartedly
And look down their nose!
These eyes search helplessly
So will they be, with me, eternally deranged.

The desperate fool

Alas! What I write with
A foolish heart and foolish hand,
Upon table and wall is meant to adorn me?

But you said: 'Fools hands smear,' –
And table and wall should be cleansed,
Until the last trace disappears!

Allow me! I will lend a hand –,
I learned to use sponge and broom
As a critic, as a waterman.

But when the work is done,
I like to see you, you over-wise,
With wisdom table and wall . . .

Rimus remedium

Oder: Wie kranke Dichter sich trösten

Aus deinem Munde,
Du speichelflüssige Hexe Zeit,
Tropft langsam Stund auf Stunde.
Umsonst, daß all mein Ekel schreit:
'Fluch, Fluch dem Schlunde
Der Ewigkeit!'

Welt-ist von Erz:
Ein glühender Stier, – der hört kein Schrein.
Mit fliegenden Dolchen schreibt der Schmerz
Mir ins Gebein:
'Welt hat kein Herz,
Und Dummheit wär's, ihr gram drum sein!'

Gieß alle Mohne,
Gieß Fieber! Gift mir ins Gehirn!
Zu lang schon prüfst du mir Hand und Stirn.
Was frägst du? Was? 'Zu welchem – Lohne?'
– Ha! Fluch der Dirn
Und ihrem Hohne!

Nein! Komm zurück!
Draußen ist's kalt, ich höre regnen –
Ich sollte dir zärtlicher begegnen?
– Nimm! Hier ist Gold: wie glänzt das Stück! –
Dich heißen 'Glück'?
Dich, Fieber, segnen? –

Rimus remedium

Or: How sick poets console themselves

Out of your mouth, you,
Spittle flowing hex of time,
Dripped slowly hour after hour.
In vain, my disgust screams:
'Curse, curse to the throat
of eternity!'

The world is from bronze:
A fiery bull – that hears no screams.
With a flying dagger, suffering writes
Into my bones:
'The world has no heart,
It is foolish to grieve about it!'

Pour all the poppies,
Pour fever! Poison into my brain!
Too long already, you examined my hands and face.
Why do you ask? What for? For which – 'A reward?'
– Ha! Curse to the whore
And her scorn!

No! Come back!
It is cold outside, I hear the rain –
Should I be more affectionate to you?
– Take it! Here is gold, how bright it shines! –
It's called 'happiness'?
Will it bless you with fever? –

Die Tür springt auf!
Der Regen sprüht nach meinem Bette!
Wind löscht das Licht, – Unheil in Hauf! –
– Wer jetzt nicht hundert *Reime* hätte,
Ich wette, wette,
Der ginge drauf!

'Mein Glück!'

Die Tauben von San Marco seh ich wieder:
Still ist der Platz, Vormittag ruht darauf.
In sanfter Kühle schick ich müßig Lieder
Gleich Taubenschwärmen in das Blau hinauf –
Und locke sie zurück,
Noch einen Reim zu hingen ins Gefieder
– mein Glück! Mein Glück!

Du stilles Himmels-Dach, blau-licht, von Seide,
Wie schwebst du schirmend ob des bunten Baus,
Den ich – was sag ich? – liebe, fürchte, *neide* . . .
Die Seele wahrlich tränk ich gern ihm aus!
Gäb ich sie je zurück? –
Nein, still davon, du Augen-Wunderweide!
– mein Glück! Mein Glück!

The door opens!
The rain is spraying my bed!
The wind blows out my light –
– Misfortune in plenty!
Who does not have a hundred rhymes,
I bet, I bet, will perish!

'My Happiness!'

I see the pigeons of San Marco again:
Still is the square, resting in mid-morning.
In gentle breeze, I muster songs as the
Pigeons begin to swarm into the blue –
And coax them back,
Still another rhyme to hang in their plumage
– My happiness! My happiness!

You silent roof of sky, light blue silk,
You gently flow over bright buildings,
That I – what am I saying – love, fear, *envy* . . .
I will gladly drink from his truthful soul!
Will I ever give it back? –
No, be quiet about it, you wondrous eye!
– My happiness! My happiness!

Du strenger Turm, mit welchem Löwendrange
Stiegst du empor hier, siegreich, sonder Müh!
Du überklingst den Platz mit tiefem Klange –:
Französisch wirst du sein *accent aigu*?
    Blieb ich gleich dir zurück,
Ich wüßte, aus welch seidenweichem Zwange . . .
– mein Glück! Mein Glück!

Fort, fort Musik! Laß erst die Schatten dunkeln
Und wachsen bis zur braunen lauen Nacht!
Zum Tone ist's zu früh am Tag, noch funkeln
Die Gold-Zieraten nicht in Rosen-Pracht,
    Noch blieb viel Tag zurück,
Viel Tag für Dichten, Schleichen, Einsam-Munkeln
– mein Glück! Mein Glück!

Nach neuen Meeren

Dorthin – *will* ich; und ich traue
Mir fortan und meinem Griff.
Offen liegt das Meer, ins Blaue
Treibt mein Genueser Schiff.

Alles glänzt mir neu und neuer,
Mittag schläft auf Raum und Zeit –:
Nur *dein* Auge – ungeheuer
Blickt mich's an, Unendlichkeit!

You, strong tower with lion's strength
Rise upwards, triumphant and without effort!
You swirl over the square with deep sounds –:
Do you have a French accent?
  That to you I will return,
I know from silky, soft compulsion . . .
– My happiness! My happiness!

Away, away music! Let the shadows first
Darken and wake to brown, lurking night!
It is too early in the sparkling day for tones,
Golden splendor is not yet in the roses,
There is still enough left of the day,
Much of the day for poetry, skulking and loneliness
– My happiness! My happiness!

To new seas

There – will I dare to go;
I will incessantly grasp it.
Open lays the blue sea,
Pursues my Genoese ship.

All looked to me new and newer,
Midday slept upon space and time –:
Only *your* eye – looked monstrous
To me – ceaselessly!

Sils-Maria

Hier saß ich, wartend, wartend, – doch auf nichts,
Jenseits von Gut und Böse, bald des Lichts
Genießend, bald des Schattens, ganz nur Spiel,
Ganz See, ganz Mittag, ganz Zeit ohne Ziel.
  Da, plötzlich, Freundin! wurde eins zu zwei –
  – Und Zarathustra ging an mir vorbei . . .

An den Mistral

Ein Tanzlied

Mistral-Wind, du Wolken-Jäger,
Trübsal-Mörder, Himmels-Feger,
Brausender, wie lieb ich dich!
Sind wir zwei nicht eines Schoßes
Erstlingsgabe, eines Loses
Vorbestimmte ewiglich?

Hier auf glatten Felsenwegen
Lauf ich tanzend dir entgegen,
Tanzend, wie du pfeifst und singst:
Der du ohne Schiff und Ruder
Als der Freiheit freister Bruder
Über wilde Meere springst.

Sils-Maria

Still I sit, waiting, waiting, – for nothing, beyond
Good and evil, close to the brilliant light,
Close to the shadow, only a game, completely sea,
Midday, and time without destination.
    There, suddenly, my friend! One became two –
    – And Zarathustra came to me . . .

To the mistral

A melody

Mistral-wind, you hunter of clouds
Dismal murderer, sky sweeper,
Sending rage, how I love you!
Are we not the first gift
Of a shot, of a chance
Destined for eternity?

Here upon the rocky, mountain path,
I laugh, dancing to you, dancing,
As you whistle and sing:
Without a ship or rudder,
Like the free'st brother of freedom
Springs across the wild sea.

Kaum erwacht, hört ich dein Rufen,
Stürmte zu den Felsenstufen,
Hin zur gelben Wand am Meer.
Heil! Da kamst du schon gleich hellen
Diamantnen Stromesschnellen
Sieghaft von den Bergen her.

Auf den ebnen Himmels-Tennen
Sah ich deine Rosse rennen,
Sah den Wagen, der dich trägt,
Sah die Hand dir selber zücken,
Wenn sie auf der Rosse Rücken
Blitzes gleich die Geißel schlägt, –

Sah dich aus dem Wagen springen,
Schneller dich hinabzuschwingen,
Sah dich wie zum Pfeil verkürzt
Senkrecht in die Tiefe stoßen, –
Wie ein Goldstrahl durch die Rosen
Erster Morgenröten stürzt.

Tanze nun auf tausend Rücken,
Wellen-Rücken, Wellen-Tücken –
Heil, wer *neue* Tänze schafft!
Tanzen wir in tausend Weisen,
Frei – sei *unsre* Kunst geheißen,
Fröhlich – *unsre* Wissenschaft!

Barely awake, I hear your call
And stormed across rocky steps
Towards the yellow painting upon the sea.
Hail! There you shone like
Diamond rays
Triumphant from the mountain tops.

Upon the smooth floor of heaven,
I saw your steed racing,
Saw your carriage that bears you,
Saw your hand strike
The whip like lightning
Across the steed's back –

I saw you jump from the carriage,
And quickly swing down,
I saw you, shortened like an arrow,
Lowered into the depth below, –
As a golden ray through roses,
First breaks this rosy dawn.

Wave crests, tricky waves
Dance upon a thousand ridges –
Hail! We create a new dance!
We will dance a thousand ways,
Free – they call our art –
Joyous – our wisdom!

Raffen wir von jeder Blume
Eine Blüte uns zum Ruhme
Und zwei Blätter noch zum Kranz!
Tanzen wir gleich Troubadouren
Zwischen Heiligen und Huren,
Zwischen Gott und Welt den Tanz!

Wer nicht tanzen kann mit Winden,
Wer sich wickeln muß mit Binden,
Angebunden, Krüppel-Greis,
Wer da gleicht den Heuchel-Hänsen,
Ehren-Tölpeln, Tugend-Gänsen,
Fort aus unsrem Paradeis!

Wirbeln wir den Staub der Straßen
Allen Kranken in die Nasen,
Scheuchen wir die Kranken-Brut!
Lösen wir die ganze Küste
Von dem Odem dürrer Brüste,
Von den Augen ohne Mut!

Jagen wir die Himmels-Trüber,
Welten-Schwärzer, Wolken-Schieber,
Hellen wir das Himmelreich!
Brausen wir . . . o aller freien
Geister Geist, mit dir zu zweien
Braust mein Glück dem Sturme gleich. –

We will pick a bloom
From every flower for our glory
And yet the two leaves wreath!
We will dance the dance of troubadours
Between saints and whores,
Between God and the dancing world!

He who cannot dance with the winds,
Who like a crippled old man
Must tie himself with binds,
Hypocrite, bumpkin
And virtuous goose –
Away from our paradise!

Whirling on the dusty road,
We scare the sick animal,
All sick in the nose!
Free are we from the shoreline
From the arid boasts of the wasteland,
And the eye without courage!

We hunt the sadness of the sky,
World blackeners! Cloud pushers!
We brighten the rule of heaven!
We roar . . . Oh! We become two
With all free, ghostly spirits who
Brighten our happiness like a storm. –

– Und daß ewig das Gedächtnis
Solchen Glücks, nimm sein Vermächtnis,
Nimm den *Kranz* hier mit hinauf!
Wirf ihn höher, ferner, weiter,
Stürm empor die Himmelsleiter,
Häng ihn – an den Sternen auf!

And he who eternally remembers
Such happiness, will never leave a legacy,
Never will the wreath be here!
He becomes higher, farther, wider,
Storms over the light heavens,
And hangs – upon the stars!

Dionysos-Dithyramben
(1888)

Dionysos Dithyrambs
(1888)

Nur Narr! Nur Dichter!

Bei abgehellter Luft,
wenn schon des Taus Tröstung
zur Erde niederquillt,
unsichtbar, auch ungehört
– denn zartes Schuhwerk trägt
der Tröster Tau gleich allen Trostmilden –
gedenkst du da, gedenkst du, heißes Herz,
wie einst du durstetest,
nach himmlischen Tränen und Taugeträufel
versengt und müde durstetest,
dieweil auf gelben Graspfaden
boshaft abendliche Sonnenblicke
durch schwarze Bäume um dich liefen,
blendende Sonnen-Glutblicke, schadenfrohe.

'Der *Wahrheit* Freier – du?' so höhnten sie –
'Nein! nur ein Dichter!'
ein Tier, ein listiges, raubendes, schleichendes,
das lügen muß,
das wissentlich, willentlich lügen muß,
nach Beute lüstern,
bunt verlarvt,
sich selbst zur Larve,
sich selbst zur Beute,
das – der Wahrheit Freier? . . .
Nur Narr! nur Dichter!
Nur Buntes redend,

Only fool, only poet!

Near an opaque sky,
Comforting dew already fell
Upon the earth,
Unseen and unheard –
– Delicate walking shoes carried
Consoling dew like all mild comfort –
Remember, remember you, hot heart,
How you once thirsted,
After heavenly tears and dew,
Scorched and tired,
Wandering upon yellow grassy paths,
Malignant evening sun rays,
Blinding rays, flew around you,
Through black trees with malicious joy.

'The free truth – you?' They scoffed –
'No! Only a poet!'
A nasty, robbing, and crawling animal,
Who must lie,
Must wisely, willingly lie,
Lusting for booty,
Colorfully disguised,
Who is the masque,
Who is booty himself,
Is *that* – the free truth? . . .
Only fool! Only poet!
Only colorful speaking,

aus Narrenlarven bunt herausredend,
herumsteigend auf lügnerischen Wortbrücken,
auf Lügen-Regenbogen
zwischen falschen Himmeln
herumschweifend, herumschleichend –
nur Narr! *nur* Dichter! . . .

Das – der Wahrheit Freier? . . .
Nicht still, starr, glatt, kalt,
zum Bilde worden,
zur Gottes-Säule,
nicht aufgestellt vor Tempeln,
eines Gottes Türwart:
nein! feindselig solchen Tugend-Standbildern,
in jeder Wildnis heimischer als in Tempeln,
voll Katzen-Mutwillens
durch jedes Fenster springend
husch! in jeden Zufall,
jedem Urwalde zuschnüffelnd,
daß du in Urwäldern
unter buntzottigen Raubtieren
sündlich gesund und schön und bunt liefest,
mit lüsternen Lefzen,
selig-höhnisch, selig-höllisch, selig-blutgierig,
raubend, schleichend, *lügend* liefest . . .

From a colorful larval fool,
Climbing upon false broken
Words and false rainbows
Between false heavens
Crawling and creeping –
Only fool! *Only* poet! . . .

That – the free truth? . . .
Not still, rigid, smooth, cold
It becomes a picture,
A pillar of God,
Not to stand in front of temples
Like a watch tower of God:
No! Hostility to such virtues
In every secret wilderness and temple,
Full of pregnant cats
Jumping through every window
Hush! In every jungle,
Smelling out every chance,
You run amidst
Colorful shaggy predators,
Happy, healthy, colorful,
With lustful lips,
Blissfully happy, polite, and bloodthirsty,
You run robbing, crawling, and deceiving . . .

Oder dem Adler gleich, der lange,
lange starr in Abgründe blickt,
in *seine* Abgründe . . .
– o wie sie sich hier hinab,
hinunter, hinein,
in immer tiefere Tiefen ringeln! –

Dann,
plötzlich,
geraden Flugs,
gezückten Zugs
auf *Lämmer* stoßen,
jach hinab, heißhungrig,
nach Lämmern lüstern,
gram allen Lamms-Seelen,
grimmig gram allem, was blickt
tugendhaft, schafmäßig, krauswollig,
dumm, mit Lammsmilch-Wohlwollen . . .

Also
adlerhaft, pantherhaft
sind des Dichters Sehnsüchte,
sind *deine* Sehnsüchte unter tausend Larven,
du Narr! du Dichter! . . .

Or, like the eagle, that long,
Long stares into the abyss,
Into *its* abyss . . .
– Oh, how it circles around in ever deeper depths! . . .
Then suddenly, straightening its flight into a
Screaming plunge, it thrusts upon the lambs! –

Then
Suddenly,
Away –
Hot hunger,
Lusts for lamb,
Grim for all lamb souls,
For everything
That looks virtuous,
Sheeply, curly,
Stupid with curly
Coated lamb's milk . . .

Thus
The poet's longings are strong as
An eagle, strong as a panther,
Your longings abide under a thousand masks,
You fool! You poet! . . .

Der du den Menschen schautest
so *Gott* als *Schaf* –,
den Gott *zerreißen* im Menschen
wie das Schaf im Menschen
und zerreißend *lachen* –

Das, das ist deine Seligkeit
eines Panthers und Adlers Seligkeit,
eines Dichters und Narren Seligkeit!' . . .

Bei abgehellter Luft,
wenn schon des Monds Sichel
grün zwischen Purpurröten
und neidisch hinschleicht,
– dem Tage feind,
mit jedem Schritte heimlich
an Rosen-Hängematten
hinsichelnd, bis sie sinken,
nachtabwärts blaß hinabsinken:

You look at men,
As *God* does a *sheep* –,
Rending God in man,
As you *rend* the sheep in men
And you *laugh* rending –

That, that is your bliss,
A panther's and an eagle's bliss,
A poet and a fool's bliss! . . .

Near an opaque sky,
The crescent moon
Crawls across crimson
And creeps enviously
– the enemy of Day,
With each secret step toward
The hanging rose gardens
Hobbling, until it sinks
With the death of the night:

so sank ich selber einstmals
aus meinem Wahrheits-Wahnsinne,
aus meinen Tages-Sehnsüchten,
des Tages müde, krank vom Lichte,
– sank abwärts, abendwärts, schattenwärts,
von einer Wahrheit
verbrannt und durstig
– gedenkst du noch, gedenkst du, heißes Herz,
wie da du durstetest? –
daß ich verbannt sei
von aller Wahrheit!
Nur Narr! *Nur* Dichter! . . .

Die Wüste wächst: weh dem, der Wüsten birgt . . .

Ha!
Feierlich!
ein würdiger Anfang!
afrikanisch feierlich!
eines Löwen würdig
oder eines moralischen Brüllaffen . . .
– aber nichts für euch,
ihr allerliebsten Freundinnen,
zu deren Füßen mir,
einem Europäer unter Palmen,
zu sitzen vergönnt ist. Sela.

So I myself once sank
From my truth and delusion,
From my Day-searching
Tired of day, sick of light,
I sank down, deeper into the shadows,
Burned and thirsty
from every truth
– Do you still remember, remember, hot heart,
How you once thirsted there?
I was banished
from all Truth!
Only fool! Only poet! . . .

The desert grows, woe to whom the desert shelters . . .

Ha!
Celebration!
A worthy start!
African celebration!
Worthy of a lion
Or a moralistic roar . . .
– But not for you,
My most lovely friends,
At whose feet,
I am permitted to sit,
A European under palm trees. Sela.

Wunderbar! wahrlich!
Da sitze ich nun,
der Wüste nahe und bereits
so ferne wieder der Wüste,
auch in nichts noch verwüstet:
nämlich hinabgeschluckt
von dieser kleinen Oasis
– sie sperrte gerade gähnend
ihr liebliches Maul auf,
das wohlriechendste aller Mäulchen:
da fiel ich hinein,
hinab, hindurch – unter euch,
ihr allerliebsten Freundinnen! Sela.

Heil, Heil jenem Walfische,
wenn er also es seinem Gaste
wohlsein ließ! – ihr versteht
meine gelehrte Anspielung? . . .
Heil seinem Bauche,
wenn es also
ein so lieblicher Oasis-Bauch war,
gleich diesem: was ich aber in Zweifel ziehe.
Dafür komme ich aus Europa,
das zweifelsüchtiger ist als alle Eheweibchen.
Möge Gott es bessern!
Amen.

Wonderful! Truthful!
There I sit now,
Close to the desert and already
So far away from the desert,
I am not only confused:
But swallowed up
by this little oasis –
– She yawned and
opened her sweet mouth
The sweetest smelling of all little mouths:
I fell into it –
here and there, under you,
My most lovely friends! Sela.

Hail! Hail! To every whale,
When he happily leaves
his guest! – Do you understand
my allusions? . . .
Hail, his belly,
when it was a
Lovely oasis-belly, no doubt:
I drifted however in doubt.
That I come from Europe is even
More doubtful than all married wives.
God make it better!
Amen.

Da sitze ich nun,
in dieser kleinsten Oasis,
einer Dattel gleich,
braun, durchsüßt, goldschwürig,
lüstern nach einem runden Mädchen-Maule,
mehr aber noch nach mädchenhaften
eiskalten schneeweißen schneidigen
Beißzähnen: nach denen nämlich
lechzt das Herz allen heißen Datteln. Sela.

Den genannten Südfrüchten
ähnlich, allzuähnlich
liege ich hier, von kleinen
Flügelkäfern
umtänzelt und umspielt,
insgleichen von noch kleineren
törichteren boshafteren
Wünschen und Einfällen, –
umlagert von euch,
ihr stummen, ihr ahnungsvollen
Mädchen-Katzen
Dudu und Suleika
– *umsphinxt*, daß ich in ein Wort
viel Gefühle stopfe
(– vergebe mir Gott
diese Sprachsünde! . . .)
– sitze hier, die beste Luft schnüffelnd,
Paradieses-Luft wahrlich,
lichte leichte Luft, goldgestreifte,

I sit here now
in this little oasis,
Like a date,
brown, sweet and golden,
Lusting after a girl's full lips,
More still however after a girl's
ice cold snow-white
Biting teeth: towards *this*
yearns the heart of all hot dates. Sela.

I lie here,
similar, all too similar
To an exotic southern fruit,
Surrounded
by small flying beetles,
dancing and playing
with me like
foolish and wicked
wishes and ideas –
surrounded by you,
silent and suspicious
Girl-cats,
Dudu and Suleika.
– *Besphinxst*, I put a lot of feeling in one word
(Forgive me God,
for this sinful speech! . . .)
I sit here, sniffing
better air, paradise skies,
Light and easy, golden striped,

so gute Luft nur je
vom Monde herabfiel,
sei es aus Zufall
oder geschah es aus Übermute?
wie die alten Dichter erzählen.
Ich Zweifler aber ziehe es in Zweifel,
dafür komme ich
aus Europa, –
das zweifelsüchtiger ist als alle Eheweibchen.
Möge Gott es bessern!
Amen.

Diese schönste Luft atmend,
mit Nüstern geschwellt gleich Bechern,
ohne Zukunft, ohne Erinnerungen,
so sitze ich hier, ihr
allerliebsten Freundinnen,
und sehe der Palme zu, wie sie, einer Tänzerin gleich,
sich biegt, und schmiegt und in der Hüfte wiegt
– man tut es mit, sieht man lange zu . . .
einer Tänzerin gleich, die, wie mir scheinen will,
zu lange schon, gefährlich lange
immer, immer nur auf *einem* Beinchen stand?
– da vergaß sie darob, wie mir scheinen will,
das *andre* Beinchen?
Vergebens wenigstens
suchte ich das vermißte
Zwillings-Kleinod
– nämlich das andre Beinchen –

good skies which
only ever fall down
from the moon,
Was it from chance or exuberance?
As the old poets say.
I doubt it.
That I come
from Europe
is even more doubtful than all married wives.
God make it better!
Amen.

Breathing this beautiful air,
With nostrils swollen like mugs
Without future, without memory
Here I sit,
my lovely dear friends,
and gaze at palm trees that bend, press
And sway their hips like dancers –
– One joins in, one looks long . . .
Is she like a dancer who for too long
Already, dangerously long, stands
Always, always only upon *one* leg?
– she forgotten
about the *other* leg?
In vain,
I searched for the twin,
The Gemini Jewel[9]
– Namely, the other leg –

in der heiligen Nähe
ihres allerliebsten, allerzierlichsten
Fächer- und Flatter- und Flitter-Röckchens.
Ja, wenn ihr mir, ihr schönen Freundinnen,
ganz glauben wollt:
sie hat es *verloren* . . .
Hu! Hu! Hu! Hu! Huh! . . .
Es ist dahin,
auf ewig dahin,
das andre Beinchen!
O schade um dies liebliche andre Beinchen!
Wo – mag es wohl weilen und verlassen trauern,
dieses einsame Beinchen?
In Furcht vielleicht vor einem
grimmen gelben blondgelockten
Löwen-Untiere? oder gar schon
abgenagt, abgeknappert –
erbärmlich! wehe! wehe! abgeknabbert! Sela.

O weint mir nicht,
weiche Herzen!
Weint mir nicht, ihr
Dattel-Herzen! Milch-Busen!
Ihr Süßholz-Herz-
Beutelchen!
Sei ein Mann, Suleika! Mut! Mut!

In holy closeness
to her lovely,
Flittering, flattering, fanning tutu.
Yes, if you can believe it,
Beautiful friends,
She has *lost* it . . .
Hu! Hu! Hu! Hu! Huh!
It has gone,
always seeking
the other leg!
Oh, what a shame, about the other lovely leg!
Where has it gone to mourn,
this other lovely leg?
In great fright from
the grim blond curly
Locks of a monstrous lion? Or perhaps
already chewed up, devoured –
Awful! Woe! Woe! Devoured! Sela.

Oh, do not cry,
Gentle heart!
Do not cry to me, your
Date-heart! Milky bosoms!
Your sweet heart –
Little booty!
Be like a man, Suleika! Courage! Courage!

Weine nicht mehr,
bleiche Dudu!
– Oder sollte vielleicht
etwas Stärkeres, Herz-Stärkendes
hier am Platze sein?
ein gesalbter Spruch?
ein feierlicher Zuspruch? . . .

Ha!
Herauf, Würde!
Blase, blase wieder,
Blasebalg der Tugend!
Ha!
Noch einmal brüllen,
moralisch brüllen,
als moralischer Löwe vor den Töchtern der Wüste
brüllen!
– Denn Tugend-Geheul,
ihr allerliebsten Mädchen,
ist mehr als alles
Europäer-Inbrunst, Luropäer-Heißhunger!
Und da stehe ich schon,
als Europäer,
ich kann nicht anders, Gott helfe mir!
Amen!

Do not cry any more,
pale Dudu!
– Or, perhaps there is
something stronger, strong as a heart,
here on the square?
A soft speech?
A celebrating speech? . . .

Ha!
Rise up!
Blow, blow again,
Bellows of virtue!
Ha!
Roar alone, roar with morality,
As a moral lion roaring,
Before the daughters of the
desert!
– Your virtuous lament,
dearest girls,
Is like all
European zeal, European hot-hunger!
And there I stand,
already a European,
I cannot do otherwise, God help me!
Amen!

Die Wüste wächst: weh dem, der Wüsten birgt!
Stein knirscht an Stein, die Wüste schlingt und
würgt.
Der ungeheure Tod blickt glühend braun
und *kaut* –, sein Leben ist sein Kaun . . .
Vergiß nicht, Mensch, den Wollust ausgeloht:
du – bist der Stein, die Wüste, bist der Tod . . .

Letzter Wille

So sterben,
wie ich ihn einst sterben sah –,
den Freund, der Blitze und Blicke
göttlich in meine dunkle Jugend warf:
– mutwillig und tief,
in der Schlacht ein Tänzer –,

unter Kriegern der Heiterste,
unter Siegern der Schwerste,
auf seinem Schicksal ein Schicksal stehend,
hart, nachdenklich, vordenklich –:

erzitternd darob, *daß* er siegte,
jauchzend darüber, daß er *sterbend* siegte –:

befehlend, indem er starb,
– und er befahl, daß man *vernichte* . . .

The desert grows, woe to whom the desert shelters!
He crunches stone upon stone, the desert chokes and
twists,
Glowing brown, he looks at monstrous death
With rumination – his life is his chewing . . .
Do not forget – Man, who quenched his lust:
You – – are stone, desert, and death . . .

Last will

So I die
as I once saw him die –
The friend, who threw lightning and
Adoration at me in my dark youth:
Pregnant and deep,
In the battle of the dancer –

The boldest amongst the warriors
Cheerful and grave under victors,
Upon his fate – a fate stands,
Hard, circumspect, anticipating –:

Trembling in the face of triumph
Jubilant that he conquers *dying* –:

Commanding, as he dies
And he commands me to *destroy* . . .

So sterben,
wie ich ihn einst sterben sah:
siegend, *vernichtend* . . .

Zwischen Raubvögeln

Wer hier hinab will,
wie schnell
schluckt den die Tiefe!
– Aber du, Zarathustra
liebst den Abgrund noch,
tust der *Tanne* es gleich? –

Die schlägt Wurzeln, wo
der Fels selbst schaudernd
zur Tiefe blickt –,
die zögert an Abgründen,
wo alles rings
hinunter will:
zwischen der Ungeduld
wilden Gerölls, stürzenden Bachs
geduldig duldend, hart, schweigsam,
einsam . . .

So I die,
like I once saw him die:
Conquering, destroying . . .

Between birds of prey

The deep will quickly swallow,
One who wants
To go downward!
But you, Zarathustra – do you still
Love the abyss –
Are you still a pine tree? –

Who has taken root where
The rock itself shudders and
Looks into the deep –
Who hesitates at the abyss,
Where everything
Goes down
Between impatient wild gushing
Streams and crushing rocks
Patiently suffering, – hard, silent,
alone . . .

Einsam!
Wer wagte es auch,
hier zu Gast zu sein,
dir Gast zu sein? . . .
Ein Raubvogel vielleicht,
der hängt sich wohl
dem standhaften Dulder
schadenfroh ins Haar,
mit irren Gelächter,
einem Raubvogel-Gelächter . . .

Wozu so standhaft?
– höhnt er grausam:
man muß Flügel haben, wenn man den
Abgrund liebt . . .
man muß nicht hängenbleiben,
wie du, Gehängter –

O Zarathustra,
grausamster Nimrod!
Jüngst Jäger noch Gottes,
das Fangnetz aller Tugend,
der Pfeil des Bösen
Jetzt –
von dir selber erjagt,
deine eigene Beute,
in dich selber eingebohrt . . .

Alone!
Who dares to
Be a guest here?
To be *your* guest? . . .
Perhaps a bird of prey
That ensnares itself happily
With steadfast suffering
Maliciously in the hair,
With mad screaming laughter,
A bird of prey laughter . . .

Why so steadfast?
– He scorns gruesomely:
One must have wings, if one
Loves the abyss . . .
One must not hang on
Like you, the hanged one! –

Oh, Zarathustra,
gruesome Nimrod!
Lately hunter, though still god,
Hunter of all virtues,
Arrow of evil! –
Now –
He hunts you, your
Own booty,
He bored into you . . .

Jetzt –
einsam mit dir,
zweisam im eignen Wissen,
zwischen hundert Spiegeln
vor dir selber falsch,
zwischen hundert Erinnerungen
ungewiß,
an jeder Wunde müd,
an jedem Froste kalt,
in eignen Stricken gewürgt,
Selbstkenner!
Selbsthenker!

Was bandest du dich
mit dein Strick deiner Weisheit?
Was locktest du dich
ins Paradies der alten Schlange?
Was schlichst du dich ein
in *dich* – in *dich*? . . .

Now –
Alone with you,
Twosome in our own knowledge,
Betwixt a hundred
False games,
Betwixt a hundred memories
Unsure,
On each tired wound
On each cold frost,
We choke on our own noose,
Self Thinker!
Self Hangman!

Why do you tie yourself
With the noose of your wisdom?
What seduces you into the
Paradise of the old snake?
Why are you one who crawls
Into yourself – into yourself? . . .

Ein Kranker nun,
der an Schlangengift krank ist;
ein Gefangner nun,
der das härteste Los zog:
im eignen Schachte
gebückt arbeitend,
in dich selber eingehöhlt,
dich selber angrabend,
unbehilflich,
steif,
ein Leichnam –,
von hundert Lasten übertürmt,
von dir überlastet,
ein *Wissender*!
ein *Selbsterkenner*!
der *weise* Zarathustra! . . .

Du suchtest die schwerste Last:
da fandest du *dich* –,
du wirfst dich nicht ab von dir . . .

Lauernd,
kauernd,
einer, der schon nicht mehr aufrecht steht!
Du verwächst mir noch mit deinem Grabe,
verwachsener Geist! . . .

A sick person now,
Sick from the poison of the snake;
A prisoner now,
With the hardest fate:
Bent down in
Your pit working,
Drawn into yourself,
Burying yourself,
Helpless,
Stiff –
A corpse –,
Burdened by a hundred burdens
Overloaded by you,
A *knower*!
A self-knower!
The wise Zarathustra! . . .

You desire the heaviest load:
There you found yourself –.
You do not throw yourself away from yourself . . .

Waiting,
Crouching,
Someone who does not stand upright anymore!
You still grow with me from
The grave, *deformed* Spirit! . . .

Und jüngst noch so stolz,
auf allen Stelzen deines Stolzes!
Jüngst noch der Einsiedler ohne Gott,
der Zweisiedler mit dem Teufel,
der scharlachne Prinz jedes Übermuts! . . .

Jetzt –
zwischen zwei Nichtse
eingekrümmt,
ein Fragezeichen,
ein müdes Rätsel –
ein Rätsel für *Raubvögel* . . .
– sie werden dich schon 'lösen'
sie hungern schon nach deiner 'Lösung',
sie flattern schon um dich, ihr Rätsel,
um dich, Gehenkter! . . .
O Zarathustra! . . .
Selbstkenner! . . .
Selbsthenker! . . .

Das Feuerzeichen

Hier, wo zwischen Meeren die Insel wuchs,
ein Opferstein jäh hinaufgetürmt,
hier zündet sich unter schwarzem Himmel
Zarathustra seine Höhenfeuer an,
Feuerzeichen für verschlagne Schiffer,
Fragezeichen für solche, die Antwort haben . . .

And still young and so proud,
upon every stilt of your pride!
Lately even a hermit without God,
the second settler with your devil,
the scarlet prince of every high feeling! . . .

Now –
crammed between
two nothings,
a question mark,
a tired riddle –
a riddle for *birds of prey* . . .
– They would already 'dissolve' you
they already crave your 'dissolution',
they flutter round you, your riddles,
around you, hanged one!
Oh, Zarathustra! . . .
Self-knower! . . .
Self-hangman! . . .

The fire sign

Here amidst the sea where a little island grew,
A sacrificial stone towers above,
It ignites itself under the black sky
On Zarathustra's holy fire, –
Fire sign for lost sailors,
Question mark for those who have the answer . . .

Diese Flamme mit weißgrauem Bauche
– in kalte Fernen züngelt ihre Gier,
nach immer reineren Höhen biegt sie den Hals –
eine Schlange gerad aufgerichtet vor Ungeduld:
dieses Zeichen stellte ich vor mich hin.

Meine Seele selber ist diese Flamme:
unersättlich nach neuen Fernen
lodert aufwärts, aufwärts ihre stille Glut.
Was floh Zarathustra vor Tier und Menschen?
Was entlief er jäh allem festen Lande?
Sechs Einsamkeiten kennt er schon –,
aber das Meer selbst war nicht genug ihm einsam,
die Insel ließ ihn steigen, auf dem Berg wurde er
zur Flamme,
nach einer *siebenten* Einsamkeit
wirft er suchend jetzt die Angel über sein Haupt.

Verschlagne Schiffer! Trümmer alter Sterne!
Ihr Meere der Zukunft! Unausgeforschte Himmel!
nach allem Einsamen werfe ich jetzt die Angel:
gebt Antwort auf die Ungeduld der Flamme,
fangt mir, dem Fischer auf hohen Bergen,
meine siebente, letzte Einsamkeit! – –

This flame with a white grey belly
– in cold distance licks your greed,
bends it neck towards always purer heights –
a snake strikes from impatience:
this sign, I placed there before me.

My soul itself is itself a flame:
insatiable for new distances
blaze upwards, upwards your still glow.
Why does Zarathustra flee from animals and man?
Why does he flee from dry land?
Six solitudes, he knows already –,
but the sea itself was not lonely enough for him,
the island lets him climb – upon the mountain he
becomes a flame,
toward his seventh solitude
he cast his fishing rod over his head.

Lost sailors! Fragments of old stars!
You, seas to the future! Unfinished heavens!
toward all the lonely I cast my rod:
I gave an answer to the impatience of the flame,
And *caught myself*, the fisher upon high mountains,
My seventh, *last* solitude! – –

Die Sonne sinkt

1.

Nicht lange durstest du noch,
verbranntes Herz!
Verheißung ist in der Luft,
aus unbekannten Mündern bläst mich's an,
– die große Kühle kommt . . .

Meine Sonne stand heiß über mir im Mittage:
seid mir gegrüßt, daß ihr kommt,
ihr plötzlichen Winde,
ihr kühlen Geister des Nachmittags!

Die Luft geht fremd und rein.
Schielt nicht mit schiefem
Verführerblick
die Nacht mich an? . . .
Bleib stark, mein tapfres Herz!
Frag nicht: warum? –

The sun sinks

1.

Not much longer will you thirst,
scorched heart!
Hope is in the air,
from an unknown mouth, it blows to me,
– the great cool comes . . .

My sun shines hot upon me at midday:
you let me know that you have come,
with your sudden wind,
you cool spirit of the afternoon!

The sky is strange and pure.
Does not the night
Squint
at me with a seducer's glance? . . .
Be brave, my strong heart!
Ask not: why? –

2.

Tag meines Lebens!
die Sonne sinkt.
Schon steht die glatte
  Flut vergüldet.
Warm atmet der Fels:
  schlief wohl zu Mittag
das Glück auf ihm seinen Mittagsschlaf? –
  In grünen Lichtern
spielt Glück noch der braune Abgrund herauf.

Tag meines Lebens!
gen Abend geht's!
Schon glüht dein Auge
  halbgebrochen,
schon quillt deines Taus
  Tränengeträufel,
schon lauft still über weiße Meere
deiner Liebe Purpur,
deine letzte zögernde Seligkeit.

2.

Day of my Life!
The sun sinks.
Already stands the smooth tide
    turning gold.
The rocks whisper warmly:
    will he sleep well at noon
will happiness befall him during his midday nap? –
    In green light
happiness still plays upon the brown abyss.

Day of my life!
Evening draws near!
Already your eyes glow,
    half-broken,
Already fall your thousand
    tear drops,
already runs upon the white sea
your purple love
your last, uncertain bliss.

3.

Heiterkeit, güldene, komm!
du des Todes
heimlichster, süßester Vorgenuß!
– Lief ich zu rasch meines Wegs?
Jetzt erst, wo der Fuß müde ward,
holt dein Blick mich noch ein,
holt dein *Glück* mich noch ein.

Rings nur Welle und Spiel.
Was je schwer war,
sank in blaue Vergessenheit
müßig steht nun mein Kahn.
Sturm und Fahrt – wie verlernt er das!
Wunsch und Hoffen ertrank,
glatt liegt Seele und Meer.

Siebente Einsamkeit!
Nie empfand ich
näher mir süße Sicherheit,
wärmer der Sonne Blick.
– Glüht nicht das Eis meiner Gipfel noch?
Silbern, leicht, ein Fisch
schwimmt nun mein Nachen hinaus . . .

3.

Laughter, golden, come!
Are you
the secret sweet foretaste of death?
– Do I run my path too rashly?
Only where my feet become tired,
your looks still catch up to me,
your happiness still catches up to me.

All around only games and waves.
What was very difficult,
sank into blue oblivion
My boat is now idle
Storms and journeys – how could he forget that!
He drank hope and longing,
smooth lies the soul and sea.

Seventh Solitude!
Never closer to myself
have I felt such sweet safety,
never warmer, the sun's rays.
– Does the ice still glow from my peak?
Silvery, light, fish
swim now upon my night . . .

Klage der Ariadne

Wer wärmt mich, wer liebt mich noch?
Gebt heiße Hände!
gebt Herzens-Kohlenbecken!
Hingestreckt, schaudernd,
Halbtotem gleich, dem man die Füße wärmt,
geschüttelt ach! von unbekannten Fiebern,
zitternd vor spitzen eisigen Frostpfeilen,
von dir gejagt, Gedanke!
Unnennbarer! Verhüllter, Entsetzlicher!
Du Jäger hinter Wolken!
Darniedergeblitzt von dir,
du höhnisch Auge, das mich aus Dunklen anblickt!
So liege ich,
biege mich, winde mich, gequält
von allen ewigen Martern,
getroffen
von dir, grausamster Jäger,
du unbekannter – *Gott* . . .

The lament of Ariadne

Who warms me? Who loves me still?
            Give hot hands!
            Give the cool basin of the heart!
Stretched out, shuddering,
Half dead, like the one who warms the feet,
I shutter, ah! from unknown fever,
shivering before the sting of icy arrows of frost,
            Hunted by you – thought!
Nameless! Frightful! Disguised!
            You hunter behind clouds!
Your eye of scorn looks
down upon me from darkness!
            So I lie,
bent and twisted, tormented
by eternal agony
            struck
by you, gruesome hunter,
you unknown – *God . . .*

Triff tiefer!
Triff einmal noch!
Zerstich, zerstich dies Herz!
Was soll dies Martern
mit zähnestumpfen Pfeilen?
Was blickst du wieder,
der Menschen-Qual nicht müde,
mit schadenfrohen Götter-Blitz-Augen?
Nicht töten willst du,
nur martern, martern?
Wozu – *mich* martern,
du schadenfroher unbekannter Gott?
Haha!
du schleichst heran
bei solcher Mitternacht? . . .
Was willst du?
Sprich!
Du drängst mich, drückst mich,
Ha! schon viel zu nahe!
Du hörst mich atmen,
du behorchst mein Herz,
du Eifersüchtiger!
– worauf doch eifersüchtig?
Weg! Weg!
wozu die Leiter?
willst du *hinein*,
ins Herz, einsteigen,
in meine heimlichsten
Gedanken einsteigen?

Strike deeper!
Strike once more!
Cut – cut this heart into pieces!
Why this torture
with blunt toothed arrows?
Do you look again, not tired of
human torment, with malicious
Lightning-god eyes?
Will you not kill –
Only torture, torture?
Why do you torture *me*,
you malicious, unknown God?
Ha, Ha!
Do you creep
up at midnight?
What do you want?
Speak!
You penetrate me, pinch me,
Ha! You are already too close!
You hear me breathe,
you listen to my heart
you are jealous!
– What are you jealous of?
Away! Away!
Why the ladder?
Will you climb *inside*
into my heart,
climb into
my secret thoughts?

Schamloser! Unbekannter! Dieb!
Was willst du dir erstehlen?
Was willst du dir erhorchen?
Was willst du dir erfoltern,
du Folterer
du – Henker-Gott!
Oder soll ich, dem Hunde gleich,
vor dir mich wälzen?
Hingebend, begeistert außer mir
dir Liebe – zuwedeln?
Umsonst!
Stich weiter!
Grausamster Stachel!
Kein Hund – dein Wild nur bin ich,
grausamster Jäger
deine stolzeste Gefangne,
du Räuber hinter Wolken . . .
Sprich endlich!
Du Blitz-Verhüllter! Unbekannter! sprich!
Was willst du, Wegelagerer, von – *mir*? . . .

Wie?
Lösegeld?
Was willst du Lösegelds?
Verlange viel – das rät mein Stolz!
und rede kurz – das rät mein andrer Stolz!
Haha!
Mich – willst du? mich?
mich – ganz? . . .

Shameless! Unknown! Thief!
What will you steal?
What will you hear?
What will you torture,
you torturer,
you – hangman God!
Or, shall I be like a dog,
wallow before you?
Devoted, enthusiastic
for your love – wagging?
For nothing!
Sting further!
Gruesome spike!
Not a dog — I am only your
wild, gruesome hunter!
I am your proud prisoner,
You robber behind clouds . . .
Finally speak!
You lightning-disguiser! Unknown! Speak!
What do you want from *me*, wanderer?

Why?
Ransom?
Why do you want ransom?
Demand much – that guessed my pride!
Speak brief – that guessed my other pride!
Ha ha!
Me – Do you want me? Me?
Me – all of me?

Haha?
Und marterst mich, Narr, der du bist,
zermarterst meinen Stolz?
Gib *Liebe* mir – wer wärmt mich noch?
          wer liebt mich noch?
gib heiße Hande,
gib Herzens-Kohlenbecken,
gib mir, der Einsamsten,
die Eis, ach! siebenfaches Eis
nach Feinden selber,
nach Feinden schmachten lehrt,
gib, ja ergib,
grausamster Feind,
mir – *dich*! . . .
Davon!
Da floh er selber,
mein einziger Genoß,
mein großer Feind,
mein Unbekannter,
mein Henker-Gott! . . .

Ha ha?
And torture me, fool, are you
destroying my pride?
Give me *love* — who warms me still?
          Who loves me still?
give hot hands,
give heart's cool basin,
give ice to me, the loneliest,
I see it! Sevenfold ice,
toward the enemy himself,
toward the enemy I learned to languish,
give, yes, give,
gruesome enemy,
yourself to me! . . .
Away!
There he flees himself,
my singular joy,
my great friend,
my unknown,
my hangman-God! . . .

Nein!
komm zurück!
Mit allen deinen Martern!
All meine Tränen laufen
zu dir den Lauf
und meine letzte Herzensflamme
dir glüht sie auf.
O komm zurück,
mein unbekannter Gott! mein *Schmerz*!
mein letztes Glück! . . .

Ein Blitz. Dionysos wird in smaragdener Schönheit sichtbar.

Dionysos:

Sei klug, Ariadne! . . .
Du hast kleine Ohren, du hast meine Ohren:
steck ein kluges Wort hinein! –
Muß man sich nicht erst hassen, wenn man sich
lieben soll? . . .
Ich bin dein Labyrinth . . .

No!
Come back!
With all your torture!
All my tears run
toward you
And the last flame of my heart
glows for you.
Oh, come back
My unknown God! My *sorrow*!
          My last happiness! . . .

Lightning – Dionysos is seen in his Emerald Beauty

Dionysos:

Be wise, Ariadne! . . . .
You have small ears, you have my ears.
Fill them with a clever word! –
Must one hate oneself first, before one can
                    love oneself?
I am your Labyrinth . . .

Ruhm und Ewigkeit

1.

Wie lange sitzest du schon
            auf deinem Mißgeschick?
Gib acht! du brütest mir noch
            ein Ei,
            ein Basilisken-Ei
aus deinem langen Jammer aus.

Was schleicht Zarathustra entlang dem Berge? –

Mißtrauisch, geschwürig, düster,
ein langer Lauerer –
aber plötzlich, ein Blitz,
hell, furchtbar, ein Schlag
gen Himmel aus dem Abgrund:
– dem Berge selber schüttelt sich
das Eingeweide . . .

Wo Haß und Blitzstrahl
eins ward, ein *Fluch* –,
auf den Bergen haust jetzt Zarathustras Zorn,
eine Wettervolke schleicht er seines Wegs.

Glory and eternity

1.

How long have you been sitting
upon your misfortune?
Take care! You lay me
An egg,
a Basilisk egg
from out of your misery.

Why does Zarathustra lurk so long on the mountain? –

Mistrusting, dark, gloomy
lying long in wait –
but suddenly – lightning,
light and horrible, a blow
against the sky from the abyss:
– the mountain itself shakes
in its entrails . . .

Where hate and lightning
become *one*, a *curse* –
upon the mountain lives Zarathustra's fury,
a weather cloud – he creeps along his way.

Verkrieche sich, wer eine letzte Decke hat!
Ins Bett mit euch, ihr Zärtlinge!
Nun rollen Donner über die Gewölbe,
nun zittert, was Gebälk und Mauer ist,
nun zucken Blitze und schwefelgelbe Wahrheiten
Zarathustra *flucht* . . .

2.

Diese Münze, mit der
alle Welt bezahlt,
Ruhm –,
mit Handschuhen fasse ich diese Münze an,
mit Ekel trete ich sie unter mich.

Wer will bezahlt sein?
Die Käuflichen . . .
Wer *feil* steht, greift
mit fetten Hinden
nach diesem Allerwelts-BlechklingKlang Ruhm!

– *Willst* du sie kaufen?
Sie sind alle käuflich
Aber biete viel!
klingle mit vollem Beutel!
– du *stärkst* sie sonst,
du stärkst sonst ihre *Tugend* . . .

Creep away into your last blanket!
Into your beds, you frail ones!
Now, thunder rolls over the vault,
now shakes timber and brick,
now lightning flashes sulphur yellow truth
          Zarathustra *curses* . . .

2.

All the world
pays with this coin,
Glory –,
With gloved hands, I touch this coin,
With disgust, I will tread upon it.

Who wants to be paid?
The shoppers . . .
Whoever is for sale, grasps
with fat hands
toward this ubiquitous Tin Kling Klang glory!

– *Will* you buy them?
They are all for sale.
Offer them a lot!
Rattle with a full purse!
– you *strengthen* them,
you strengthen their *virtue* . . .

Sie sind alle tugendhaft.
Ruhm und Tugend – das reimt sich.
Solange die Welt lebt,
zahlt sie Tugend-Geplapper
mit Ruhm-Geklapper –,
die Welt *lebt* von diesem Lärm . . .

Vor allen Tugendhaften
              will ich schuldig sein,
schuldig heißen mit jeder groben Schuld!
Vor allen Ruhms-Schalltrichtern
wird mein Ehrgeiz zum Wurm –,
unter solchen gelüstet's mich,
der *Niedrigste* zu sein . . .

Diese Münze, mit der
alle Welt bezahlt,
Ruhm –,
mit Handschuhen fasse ich diese Münze an,
mit Ekel trete ich sie *unter* mich.

3.

Still! –
Von großen Dingen – ich *sehe* Großes!
soll man schweigen
oder groß reden:
rede groß, meine entzückte Weisheit!

They are all virtuous.
Glory and virtue – that rhymes.
So long as the world still lives,
it pays virtue-chatter,
with fame-clatter –,
the world *lives* by that noise . . .

Before all virtuousness
            I want to be guilty,
called guilty with every great guilt!
Before all glory-trickery,
my ambition is to become like a worm –
under such lust,
I become the *lowest* . . .

With this coin
the whole world pays,
Glory –
with gloved hands, I touch this coin
with disgust, I tread upon it.

3.

Still! –
From great things – I *see* greatness! –
shall one be silent
or speak loudly:
speak loudly, my blissful wisdom!

Ich sehe hinauf –
dort rollen Lichtmeere:
o Nacht, o Schweigen, o totenstiller Lärm! . . .
Ich sehe ein Zeichen –,
aus fernsten Fernen
sinkt langsam funkelnd ein Sternbild gegen mich . . .

4.

Höchstes Gestirn des Seins!
Ewiger Bildwerke Tafel!
Du kommst zu mir?
Was keiner erschaut hat,
deine stumme Schönheit –
wie? sie flieht vor meinen Blicken nicht? –

Schild der Notwendigkeit!
Ewiger Bildwerke Tafel!
– aber du weißt es ja:
was alle hassen,
was allein *ich* liebe:
– daß *du ewig* bist!
daß du *notwendig* bist! –
meine Liebe entzündet
sich ewig nur an der Notwendigkeit.

I look up –
there rolls the light of the sea:
Oh night, oh silence, Oh deathly still noise! . . .
I see the sign –
from far away
sinks slowly the light of a sparkling star to me . . .

4.

Highest star of being!
Eternal work of art!
You come to me?
Nobody has seen
your clumsy beauty –
How? Does she flee not from my gaze? –

Shield of necessity!
Eternal work of art!
– but you know it yes:
what I hate.
what I love:
– that you are eternal!
that you are *necessary*!
My love inflames itself
eternal only in necessity.

Schild der Notwendigkeit!
Höchstes Gestirn des Seins!
– das kein Wunsch erreicht,
– das kein Nein befleckt,
ewiges Ja des Seins,
ewig bin ich dein Ja:
denn ich liebe dich, o Ewigkeit! – –

Von der Armut des Reichsten

Zehn Jahre dahin –,
kein Tropfen erreichte mich,
kein feuchter Wind, kein Tau der Liebe
– ein *regenloses* Land . . .
Nun bitte ich meine Weisheit,
nicht geizig zu werden in dieser Dürre:
ströme selber über, träufle selber Tau,
sei selber Regen der vergilbten Wildnis!

Einst hieß ich die Wolken
fortgehn von meinen Bergen, –
einst sprach ich ‘mehr Licht, ihr Dunklen!’
Heut locke ich sie, daß sie kommen:
macht Dunkel um mich mit euren Eutern!
– ich will euch melken,
ihr Kühe der Höhe!
Milchwarme Weisheit, süßen Tau der Liebe
ströme ich über das Land.

Shield of necessity!
Highest star of humanity!
– that does not reach its desire,
– that does not flee the impossible,
eternal Yes of Being
eternally I am your yes,
because I love you, oh Eternity! – –

The poverty of the rich

Ten years gone –,
not a drop reached me,
no moist wind, no dew of love
– a *rainless* land . . .
Now I am begging my wisdom
not to become mean in this aridity:
stream over yourself, drip dew over yourself,
be yourself the rain in the barren wilderness!

Once I told the clouds
to go away from my mountains, –
once I spoke: 'More light, you dark ones!'
Today I entice them, so that they come:
make dark around me with your udders!
– I will milk you,
you cow of the heights!
Milky warm wisdom, sweet dew of love
I stream over the land.

Fort, fort, ihr Wahrheiten,
die ihr düster blickt!
Nicht will ich auf meinen Bergen
herbe ungeduldige Wahrheiten sehn.
Vom Lächeln vergüldet
nahe mir heut die Wahrheit,
von der Sonne gesüßt, von der Liebe gebräunt, –
eine *reife* Wahrheit breche ich allein vom Baum.

Heut Strecke ich die Hand aus
nach den Locken des Zufalls,
klug genug, den Zufall
einem Kinde gleich zu führen, zu überlisten.
Heut will ich gastfreundlich sein
gegen Unwillkommnes,
gegen das Schicksal selbst will ich nicht stachlicht sein,
– Zarathustra ist kein Igel.

Meine Seele,
unersättlich mit ihrer Zunge,
an alle guten und schlimmen Dinge hat sie schon
geleckt,
in jede Tiefe tauchte sie hinab.
Aber immer gleich dem Korke,
immer schwimmt sie wieder obenauf,
sie gaukelt wie Öl über braune Meere:
dieser Seele halber heißt man mich den Glücklichen.

Away, away your truth,
your gloomy look!
I will not see bitter, impatient
truth upon my mountain.
From golden laughter
truth draws near to me tonight,
sweetened by sun, tanned by love, –
I will pick a *ripe* truth from the tree.

Today I stretch out my hand
toward the lures of chance,
Clever enough, and random
like a child, to lead and outwit chance.
Today I will be hospitable
against the unwelcome,
against fate itself I will not be lightly pricked,
– Zarathustra is no hedgehog!

My soul,
insatiable with her tongue,
all good and bad things she has already
licked,
into every depth she has already dived,
But always like a cork,
always she swims up to the surface,
she sways like oil over the brown sea:
In this light, they call me the lucky one.

Wer sind mir Vater und Mutter?
Ist nicht mir Vater Prinz Überfluß
und Mutter das stille Lachen?
Erzeugte nicht dieser beiden Ehebund
mich Rätseltier,
mich Lichtunhold,
mich Verschwender aller Weisheit, Zarathustra?

Krank heute vor Zärtlichkeit,
ein Tauwind,
sitzt Zarathustra wartend, wartend auf seinen
Bergen, –
im eignen Safte
süß geworden und gekocht,
unterhalb seines Gipfels,
unterhalb seines Eises,
müde und selig,
ein Schaffender an seinem siebenten Tag.

– Still!
Eine Wahrheit wandelt über mir
einer Wolke gleich, –
mit unsichtbaren Blitzen trifft sie mich.
Auf breiten langsamen Treppen
steigt ihr Glück zu mir:
komm, komm, geliebte Wahrheit!

Who are my father and mother?
Is not my father, Prince Excess
and my mother, Quiet Laughter?
Did not this marriage produce
me, the riddler,
me, the monstrous light,
me, the spendthrift of all wisdom, Zarathustra?

Sick for the affection
of a dewy wind,
Zarathustra sits waiting, waiting, upon his
mountain, –
in his juices, he
becomes cooked and sweet,
underneath his peak
underneath his ice
tired and blissful,
a creator on his seventh day.

– Silence!
A truth wanders over me
like a cloud, –
with unforeseen lightning, it strikes me.
Upon wide, slow stairs
climbs your luck to me:
come, come, beloved Truth!

– Still!
Meine Wahrheit ist's! –
Aus zögernden Augen,
aus samtenen Schaudern
triff mich ihr Blick,
lieblich, bös, ein Mädchenblick . . .
Sie erriet meines Glückes *Grund*,
sie erriet *mich* – ha! was sinnt sie aus? –
Purpurn lauert ein Drache
im Abgrunde ihres Mädchenblicks.

– Still! Meine Wahrheit *redet*! –

Wehe dir, Zarathustra!
Du siehst aus, wie einer,
der Gold verschluckt hat:
man wird dir noch den Bauch aufschlitzen! . . .

Zu reich bist du,
du Verderber vieler!
Zu viele machst *du* neidisch,
zu viele machst du arm . . .
Mir selber wirft dein Licht Schatten –,
es fröstelt mich: geh weg, du Reicher,
geh, Zarathustra, weg aus deiner Sonne! . . .

– Silence!
It is *my* truth! –
From reluctant eyes,
from silken shudders,
Her gaze strikes me,
Lovely, naughty, a girl's look . . .
She guessed the *reason* for my happiness,
she guessed *me* – Ha! What is she thinking? –
Purple lurks a dragon
in this abyss of girlish looks.

– Silence! My truth *speaks*! –

Woe to you, Zarathustra!
You look like one
who has swallowed gold:
one will have to cut open your belly! . . .

You are too rich,
you destroyer of so much!
Too many – you have made jealous
too many – you have made poor . . .
The shadow of your light is thrown to me –,
it freezes me: go away – – – you rich one,
Go, Zarathustra, away from your sun! . . .

Du möchtest schenken, wegschenken deinen Überfluß,
aber du selber bist der Überflüssigste!
Sei klug, du Reicher!
Verschenke dich selber erst, o Zarathustra!

Zehn Jahre dahin –,
und kein Tropfen erreichte dich?
kein feuchter Wind? kein Tau der Liebe?
Aber wer *sollte* dich auch lieben,
du Überreicher?
Dein Glück macht rings trocken,
macht arm an Liebe –
ein *regenloses* Land . . .

Niemand dankt dir mehr.
Du aber dankst jedem,
der von dir nimmt:
daran erkenne ich dich,
du Überreicher,
du *Ärmster* aller Reichen!

Du opferst dich, dich *quält* dein Reichtum –,
du gibst dich ab,
du schonst dich nicht, du liebst dich nicht:
die große Qual zwingt dich allezeit,
die Qual *übervoller* Scheuern, *übervollen* Herzens –
aber niemand dankt dir mehr . . .

You would like to give away your excess,
but you are yourself this excess!
Be clever, you rich one!
Give yourself away first, oh, Zarathustra!

Ten years gone –,
And no drops reach you?
No moist wind? No dew of love?
But, who will love you,
you, *overrich*?
Your luck makes everything dry,
makes love poor –
a *rainless* land! . . .

Nobody thanks you anymore.
But you thank everyone,
who takes from you:
I know you because of this,
you, *overrich*,
you poorest of all the rich!

You sacrifice yourself, your riches torture you –,
you give yourself away,
you pursue yourself not, you love yourself not:
your great torment compels you all the time,
the torment of *overfull* fear, *overfull* hearts –
but, no one thanks you any more . . .

Du mußt *ärmer* werden,
weiser Unweiser!
willst du geliebt sein.
Man liebt nur die Leidenden,
man gibt Liebe nur dem Hungernden:
verschenke dich selbst erst, o Zarathustra!

– Ich bin deine Wahrheit . . .

You must become *poorer*,
Wise, unwise one!
You want to be loved.
One loves only the afflicted
one only gives love to the hungry:
give yourself away first, oh Zarathustra!

– I am your truth . . .

Aus dem umkreis der Dionysos-Dithyramben (1882–1888)

Through the circle of Dionysos Dithyrambs (1882–1888)

1.

Zürnt mir nicht, daß ich schlief:
ich war nur müde, ich war nicht tot.
Meine Stimme klang böse;
aber bloß Schnarchen und Schnaufen
war's, der Gesang eines Müden:
kein Willkomm dem Tode,
keine Grabes-Lockung.

2.

Noch rauscht die Wetterwolke:
aber schon hängt
glitzernd, still, schwer
Zarathustras Reichtum über die Felder hin.

3.

Auf Höhen bin ich heimisch,
nach Höhen verlangt mich nicht.
Ich liebe die Augen nicht empor;
ein Niederschauender bin ich,
einer, der segnen muß:
alle Segnenden schauen nieder . . .

4.

Ist für solchen Ehrgeiz
diese Erde nicht zu klein?

1.

Do not be angry that I slept:
I was only tired – I was not dead
My voice sounds evil; but it is
only blowing snorts and snores,
the melody of tired ones:
no welcome to death,
no seduction to the grave.

2.

The weather cloud rushes still:
but Zarathustra's riches already
hang glittering, quiet,
heavy, over the fields.

3.

I feel at home upon the heights,
but I do not long toward the heights.
I do not lift my eyes upward;
I look down, as
one who must bless:
blessing ones – always look down . . .

4.

Is the world not too small
for such ambition?

5.

Alles gab ich weg,
all mein Hab und Gut:
Nichts bleibt mir mehr zurück
als du, große Hoffnung!

6.

Was geschieht? fällt das Meer?
Nein, mein Land wächst!
Eine neue Glut hebt es empor!

7.

Mein Jenseits Glück!
Was heut mir Glück ist,
wirft Schatten in seinem Lichte.

8.

Diese heitere Tiefe!
Was Stern sonst hieß,
zum Flecken wurde es.

9.

Ihr steifen Weisen,
mir ward alles Spiel.

5.

All I gave away –
all my possessions and goods:
Nothing remains to me,
except you, my great hope!

6.

What happened? Did the sea fall?
No, my land grows!
A new glow lifts it upwards!

7.

My beyond-happiness!
What is happiness for me today
I throw shadows into his light.

8.

This bright depth!
It was once called a star,
it became a stain.

9.

You, stiff, wise ones,
you all become a game to me.

10.

Brause, Wind, brause!
Nimm alles Behagen von mir!

11.

Damit begann ich:
ich verlernte das Mitgefühl mit *mir*!

12.

Trümmer von Sternen:
aus diesen Trümmern baute ich eine Welt.

13.

Nicht, daß du Götzen umwarfst:
daß du den Götzendiener in *dir* umwarfst,
das war dein Mut.

10.

Roar, wind, roar!
Take all comfort from me!

11.

With that, I began:
I unlearned sympathy with *myself*!

12.

Wreckage of stars:
I built a world from this wreckage.

13.

Not that you cast away idols: that you
cast away idol-worship in yourself,
that was your courage.

14.

Da stehn sie da,
die schweren granitnen Katzen,
die Werte aus Urzeiten:
wehe, wie willst du *die* umwerfen?
....
Kratzkatzen
mit gebundenen Pfoten,
da sitzen sie
und blicken Gift.

15.

An dieser steinernen Schönheit
kühlt sich mein heißes Herz.

16.

Wahrheiten, die noch kein Lächeln
vergüldet hat,
grüne herbe ungeduldige Wahrheiten
sitzen um mich herum.
....
Wahrheiten für unsere Füße!
Wahrheiten, nach denen sich tanzen läßt!

14.

They stand there,
heavy granite cats,
treasures of ancient times:
Woe, how will you throw them down?
....
Fighting cats
with bandaged paws,
there they sit
with looks of poison.

15.

On their stony beauty
my hot heart cools itself.

16.

Truth that still has no
golden laughter,
green, bitter, impatient truth
that hops around me here.
....
Truth for our feet!
Truth you can dance to!

17.

Ein Blitz wurde meine Weisheit;
mit diamantenem Schwerte durchhieb sie mir jede
Finsternis!

18.

Dieses höchste Hindernis,
den Gedanken der Gedanken,
wer schuf ihn sich?
Das Leben selber schuf sich
sein höchstes Hindernis:
über seinen Gedanken selber springt es
nunmehr hinweg.
....
An diesem Gedanken
ziehe ich alle Zukunft.

19.

Ein Gedanke,
jetzt noch heiß-flüssig, Lava:
aber jede Lava baut
um sich selbst eine Burg,
jeder Gedanke erdrückt
sich zuletzt mit 'Gesetzen'.

17.

Lightning becomes my wisdom;
with a diamond sword it slashes me through every
darkness!

18.

This highest obstacle,
the thought of thoughts,
she creates herself?
Life herself creates
her highest obstacle:
upon her own thoughts she leaps,
and holds fast.
....
With these thoughts,
I draw every future.

19.

A thought,
now still hot flowing lava:
but each lava builds
around itself a castle,
each thought crushes
itself finally with 'Law'.

20.

So ist's jetzt mein Wille:
und seit das mein Wille ist,
geht alles mir auch nach Wunsche –
dies war meine letzte Klugheit:
ich wollte *das*, was ich muß:
damit zwang ich mir jedes 'Muß' . . .
seitdem gibt es für mich kein 'Muß' . . .

21.

Rate, Rätselfreund,
wo weilt jetzt meine Tugend?
Sie lief mir davon,
sie fürchtete die Arglist
meiner Angeln und Netze.

22.

Ein Wolf selbst zeugte für mich
und sprach: 'du heulst besser noch als wir Wölfe.'

23.

Tauschen –
das ist im Kriege alles.
Die Haut des Fuchses:
sie ist mein heimliches Panzerhemd.

20.

So it is now my intention:
and since this is my intention,
all goes according to my wishes –
this was my last cleverness:
I wanted *that*, which I must want
with it, I compelled each 'must' . . .
since then, there was no 'must' for me . . .

21.

Guess, riddling friend,
where is my virtue now?
She ran away from me,
she was frightened by the
malice of my angling and nets.

22.

A wolf himself testified for me,
and said: 'You howl better than us wolves.'

23.

Deception –
is everything in war.
The fox skin:
is my secret armored shirt.

24.

Wo Gefahr ist,
da bin ich daheim,
da wachse ich aus der Erde.

25.

Nach neuen Schätzen wühlen wir,
wir neuen Unterirdischen:
gottlos schien es den Alten einst,
nach Schätzen aufzustören der Erde Eingeweide;
von neuem gibt es solche Gottlosigkeit:
hört ihr nicht aller Tiefen Bauchgrimmen-Gepolter?

26.

Die Sphinx

Hier sitzest du, unerbittlich
wie meine Neubegier,
die mich zu dir zwang:
wohlan, Sphinx,
ich bin ein Fragender, gleich dir;
dieser Abgrund ist uns gemeinsam –
es wäre möglich, daß wir mit *einem* Munde redeten!

24.

Where danger is,
I am at home,
there I grow out of the earth.

25.

Toward new treasures we dig
we, the new men under the earth:
it seemed godless in old times
to dig up treasures from the earth;
new times give you this godlessness:
can you not hear the grim belly din of everything deep?

26.

The Sphinx

You sit, inexorable
just as the curiosity that
forced me to you:
charming Sphinx,
I am a questioner, like you;
this abyss is our domain –
is it possible that we speak with *one* mouth?

27.

Ich bin einer, dem man Schwüre schwört:
schwört mir dies!

28.

Nach Liebe suchen – und immer die *Larven*,
die verfluchten Larven finden und zerbrechen müssen!

29.

Liebe ich euch?
So liebt der Reiter sein Pferd:
es tragt ihn zu seinem Ziele.

30.

Sein Mitleid ist hart,
sein Liebesdruck zerdrückt:
gebt einem Riesen nicht die Hand!

31.

Ihr fürchtet mich?
Ihr fürchtet den gespannten Bogen?
Wehe, es könnte einer seinen Pfeil darauf legen!

32.

'Neue Nächte hülltest du um dich,
neue Wüsten erfand dein Löwenfuß.'

27.

I am one who swears oaths:
swear this to me!

28.

I search for love – – and always the *mask*,
I must find, and break the cursed larva!

29.

Do I love you?
So, the rider loves his horse:
it carries him to his destination.

30.

His sympathy is hard,
his loving touch crushes:
do not give your hand to a giant!

31.

You are afraid of me?
You are frightened of my taut bow?
Woe, if he can lay his arrow upon it!

32.

'You wrap new nights around me,
your lion's foot invents new deserts.'

33.

Ich bin nur ein Worte-Macher:
was liegt an Worten!
Was liegt an mir!

34.

Ach, meine Freunde:
wohin ist, was man 'gut' hieß!
Wohin sind alle 'Guten'!
Wohin, wohin ist die Unschuld aller dieser Lügen!
....
Alles heiße ich gut,
Laub und Gras, Glück, Segen und Regen.

35.

Nicht an seinen Sünden und großen Torheiten:
an seiner Vollkommenheit litt ich, als ich
am meisten am Menschen litt.

36.

'Der Mensch ist böse',
so sprachen noch alle Weisesten –
mir zum Troste.

33.

I am only a word-maker,
what matters words!
what matters me!

34.

I see it, my friends
wherein what one calls 'good'!
whither are all 'Good'!
wherein, whither is the innocence of all these lies!
………………………………………………..
I call everything good,
Foliage, grass, happiness, blessing and rain.

35.

I suffered not from his sins and foolishness:
I suffered from his perfection,
as I suffered from mankind.

36.

'Man is evil',
so speak all the wise –
to console me.

37.

Und nur wenn ich mir selbst zur Last bin,
fallt *ihr* mir schwer!

38.

Zu bald schon
lache ich wieder:
ein Feind hat
wenig bei mir gutzumachen.

39.

Leutselig (bin ich) gegen Mensch und Zufall,
leutselig mit jedermann, auch mit Gräsern noch:
ein Sonnenfleck an winterlichen Hängen . . .
feucht vor Zärtlichkeit,
ein Tauwind verschneiten Seelen:
....
Hochmütig gegen kleine
Vorteile: wo ich der Krämer
lange Finger sehe,
da gelüstet's mich sofort,
den kürzere zu ziehn –
so will's mein spröder Geschmack von mir.

40.

Ein fremder Atem haucht und faucht mich an:
bin ich ein Spiegel, der drob trübe wird?

37.

And only when I am a burden to myself,
you are heavy to me!

38.

Too soon already,
I laugh again:
an enemy has
little to do for me.

39.

I am affable with man and chance,
with everyone and the grass:
sunspots on wintry slopes . . .
moist with tenderness,
dew winds cover the soul with snow:
....
I am haughty against little
favors: I see the long finger
of the shopkeeper,
I am tempted to
pull the shortest –
So wills my fragile taste.

40.

A strange breeze breathes and hisses upon me,
am I a mirror that becomes gloomy above?

41.

Kleine Leute,
zutraulich, offenherzig,
aber niedere Türen:
nur Niedriges tritt durch sie ein
....
Wie komme ich durch das Stadttor?
ich verlernte es, unter Zwergen zu leben!

42.

Meine Weisheit tat der Sonne gleich:
ich wollte ihnen Licht sein,
aber ich habe sie geblendet;
die Sonne meiner Weisheit stach
diesen Fledermäusen
die Augen aus . . .

43.

'Schwürzres und Schlimmres schautest du als irgendein
Seher:
durch die Wollust der Hölle ist noch kein Weiser
gegangen.'

44.

Zurück! Ihr folgt mir zu nah auf dem Fuße!
Zurück, daß meine Wahrheit euch nicht den Kopf
zertrete!

41.

Small people,
friendly and open hearted,
but small doors:
only the smallest will enter
....
How will I get through the city door?
I forgot how to live under dwarves!

42.

My wisdom acts like the sun:
I would like to be their light
but I have blinded them;
the sun of my wisdom pokes
out the eyes
of this bat . . .

43.

'Darkness and cruelty is shown to you as an
onlooker:
through the lusts of hell the wise man still
does not go!'

44.

Go back! You follow too close on my feet!
Go back, so that my knowledge does not trample
upon your head!

45.

'Zur Hölle geht, wer deine Wege geht!' –
Wohlan! Zu meiner Hölle
will ich den Weg mir mit guten Sprüchen pflastern.

46.

Euer Gott, sagt ihr mir,
ist ein Gott der Liebe?
Der Gewissensbiß
ist ein Gottesbiß,
ein Biß aus Liebe?

47.

Der Affe seines Gottes –
willst du nur der Affe deines Gottes sein?

48.

Sie kauen Kiesel,
sie liegen auf dem Bauche
vor kleinen runden Sachen;
sie beten alles an, was nicht umfällt, –
diese letzten Gottesdiener,
(die Wirklichkeits-)Gläubigen!

45.

'To hell goes who goes your way!' –
Carry on! To my hell,
will I plaster my way with good rhymes.

46.

Your god – you say to me,
is the god of love?
A conscience bite
is a godly bite,
a bite from love?

47.

The ape of his God –
will you only be an ape of your God?

48.

They chew grit,
they lie upon their bellies
before small round things;
they pray to everything that has not fallen –
these last servants of God,
(the true) believers!

49.

Ohne Weiber, schlecht genährt
und ihren Nabel beschauend,
– des Schmutze Bilder,
Übelriechende!
Also erfanden sie sich die Wollust Gottes.

50.

Sie haben ihren Gott aus Nichts geschaffen:
was Wunder: nun ward er ihnen zunichte.

51.

Ihr höheren Menschen – es gab schon
denkendere Zeiten, zerdachtere Zeiten,
als unser Heut und Gestern ist.

52.

Diese Zeit ist wie ein krankes Weib –
laßt sie nur schreien, rasen, schimpfen
und Tisch und Teller zerbrechen! . . .

53.

Ihr Verzweifelnden! Wie viel Mut
macht ihr denen, die euch zuschauen!

49.

Without women, badly fed,
and looking at their navels
– dirty pictures,
foul smelling!
Thus, they invent the voluptuousness of God.

50.

They created their God from nothing:
what a wonder: now he becomes their ruin.

51.

You higher men – there are already
thoughtful times, thought destroying times,
our yesterday and today.

52.

Time is like a sick woman –
Let her scream, lament, grumble
And break the table and the chairs! . . .

53.

You, desperate ones! How much courage
you give to those who only watch!

54.

Steigt ihr?
Ist es wahr, daß ihr steigt,
ihr höheren Menschen?
Werdet ihr nicht, verzeiht,
dem Balle gleich
in die Höhe *gedrückt*
– durch euer Niedrigstes? . . .
flieht ihr nicht vor euch, ihr Steigenden? . . .

55.

Ach, daß du glaubtest
verachten zu müssen,
wo nur du verzichtetest!

56.

Und alle *Männer* sagen diesen Kehrreine:
Nein! Nein! Dreimal Nein!
Was Himmel-Bimmel-bam-bam!
Wir *wollen* nicht ins Himmelreich –
das Erdenreich soll unser sein!

57.

Der Wille erlöst.
Wer nichts zu tun hat,
dein macht ein Nichts zu schaffen.

54.

You climb?
Is it true that you climb,
you higher men?
Are you not forgiven,
Quashed like a ball
into the height
– though your humility?
Do you not *flee* from yourselves, you climbers? . . .

55.

I see that you
must truly despise,
where once you only renounced!

56.

And all *men* say this rhyme:
No! No! Three times No!
What heavenly tinkling ding dong!
We do not want a rule of heaven –
we want to be the rule of the earth.

57.

The will redeems.
Who has nothing to do
will create a nothingness.

58.

Du hältst es nicht mehr aus,
dein herrisches Schicksal?
Liebe es, es bleibt dir keine Wahl!

59.

Das allein erlöst von allem Leiden –
(– wähle nun!):
den schnellen Tod
oder die lange Liebe.

60.

Seines Todes ist man gewiß:
warum wollte man nicht heiter sein?

61.

Den schlimmsten Einwand
ich verbarg ihn euch – das Leben wird langweilig:
werft es weg, damit es euch wieder schmackhaft wird!

62.

Einsame Tage,
ihr wollt auf tapferen Füßen gehen!

58.

You cannot bear your
ruling fate anymore?
Love it, it remains your only choice!

59.

That alone redeems all suffering –
(– choose now!):
a quick death
or, a long love.

60.

I am sure of my death:
why should I not be happy?

61.

I concealed the worst objection from you –
that life becomes boring: throw it away,
with that, it will become tasty again!

62.

Lonely days,
you want to walk on brave feet!

63.

Die Einsamkeit
pflanzt nicht: sie reift . . .
Und dazu noch mußt du die Sonne
zur Freundin haben.

64.

Du mußt wieder ins Gedränge:
im Gedränge wird man glatt und hart.
Die Einsamkeit mürbt,
die Einsamkeit verdirbt . . .

65.

Wenn den Einsamen
die große Furcht anfällt,
wenn er läuft und läuft
und weiß selber nicht wohin?
wenn Stürme hinter ihm brüllen,
wenn der Blitz gegen ihn zeugt,
wenn seine Höhle mit Gespenstern
ihn fürchten macht . . .

66.

Wetterwolken – – was liegt an euch?
für uns, die freien, luftigen, lustigen Geister!

63.

Loneliness
does not grow: it ripens . . .
And you must still have a friend –
the sun.

64.

You must go again into the crowds:
you will become smooth and hard.
Loneliness makes you morose,
loneliness corrupts you.

65.

When the lonely one
has a devastating fright
when he runs and runs and
does not know where to go?
when storms roar behind him
when lightning strikes him,
when his cave full of ghosts
frightens him . . .

66.

Weather clouds – – – what matter they to you?
for us, the free, airy and merry spirits!

67.

Wirf dein Schweres in die Tiefe!
Mensch, vergiß! Mensch, vergiß!
Göttlich ist des Vergessens Kunst!
Willst du fliegen,
willst du in Höhen heimisch sein:
wirf dein Schwerstes in das Meer!
Hier ist das Meer, wirf *dich* ins Meer!
Göttlich ist des Vergessens Kunst!

68.

Bist du so neugierig?
Kannst du um die Ecke sehn?
Man muß, um *das* zu sehn,
Augen auch hinter dem Kopfe haben!

69.

Sich hinaus! sieh nicht zurück!
Man geht zugrunde,
wenn man immer zu den Gründen geht.

70.

Den Verwegnen
hüte dich zu warnen!
Um der Warnung willen
Läuft er in jeden Abgrund noch.

67.

Throw your burden into the depths!
Man, forget! Man, forget!
Godly is the art of forgetfulness!
You want to fly –
to be at home in heights:
throw your burden into the sea!
Here is the sea – throw yourself into the sea!
Godly is the art of forgetfulness!

68.

Are you curious?
Can you see around the corner?
One must have eyes at the back of one's head,
To see around *that*!

69.

Look ahead! Do not look back!
One goes to the ground
when he always goes after grounds.

70.

Be warned
guard against the daring!
Around the warning, he still wants to
Run into every abyss.

71.

Was warf er sich auf seiner Höhe?
was verführte ihn?
Das Mitleiden mit allem Niedrigen verführte ihn:
nun liegt er da, zerbrochen, unnütz, kalt –

72.

Wohin er ging? wer weiß es?
Aber gewiß ist, daß er unterging.
Ein Stern erlosch im öden Raum:
öde ward der Raum . . .

73.

Was man nicht hat,
aber nötig hat,
das soll man sich nehmen;
so nahm ich mir das gute Gewissen.

74.

Wer wäre das, der Recht dir geben könnte?
So *nimm* dir Recht!

71.

Why did he throw himself from his height?
what provoked him?
Sympathy with the humble provoked him:
now he lies there, broken, useless, cold –

72.

Where did he go? Who knows?
But it is certain that he went down.
A star expired in the barren room:
barren became the room . . .

73.

What one has not,
but what one needs,
one shall take;
so I took my good conscience.

74.

Who can give you a right?
So *take* your right!

75.

Ihr Wellen!
ihr Wunderlichen! ihr zürnt gegen mich?
ihr rauscht zornig auf?
Mit meinem Ruder schlage ich
eurer Torheit auf den Kopf.
Diesen Nachen –
ihr selber tragt ihn noch zur Unsterblichkeit!

76.

Was um euch wohnt,
das wohnt sich bald euch ein:
Gewöhnung wird daraus.
Wo lang du sitzest,
da wachsen Sitten.

77.

Als keine neue Stimme mehr redete,
machtet ihr aus alten Worten
ein Gesetz:
wo Leben *erstarrt*, türmt sich das Gesetz.

78.

Dergleichen mag nicht widerlegbar sein:
wäre es schon deshalb wahr?
Oh, ihr Unschuldigen!

75.

You waves!
You enchanters! You are angry with me?
You roar with rage?
With my rudder, I strike
your folly upon the head.
This night –
you still carry me into immortality!

76.

What lives around you,
you soon yourself live:
it becomes a habitat,
where you sit long,
habits will grow.

77.

When no new voices speak anymore,
you make from old words
a new law:
where life grows rigid, the law towers.

78.

Such will not be refuted:
is it therefore already true?
Oh, you innocents!

79.

Bist du stark?
stark als Esel? stark als Gott?
Bist du stolz?
stolz genug, daß du deiner Eitelkeit
dich nicht zu schämen weißt?

80.

Hüte dich,
sei nicht der Paukenschläger
deines Schicksals!
Geh aus dem Weg
allen Bumbums des Ruhms!
....
nicht zu früh erkannt:
einer, der seinen Ruf *aufgespart* hat.

81.

Willst du in Dornen greifen?
Schwer büßen's deine Finger.
Greife nach einem Dolch!

82.

Bist du zerbrechlich?
So hüte dich vor *Kindshänden*!
Das Kind kann nicht leben,
wenn es nichts zerbricht . . .

79.

Are you strong?
Strong as an ass? Strong as God?
Are you proud?
Proud enough not to know
How to be ashamed of your vanity?

80.

Be on your guard,
do not be the drum beater
of your fate!
Go away from
all the bang-bang of glory!
....
not too early did he see:
one who had been *sparing* with his cry.

81.

Do you grasp in the thorns?
Heavy pays your finger.
Reach for a dagger!

82.

Are you breakable?
Beware of the *child's hand*!
The child cannot live
if it cannot break . . .

83.

Schone, was solch zarte Haut hat!
Was willst du den Flaum
von solchen Dingen schaben?

84.

Deine großen Gedanken,
die aus dem Herzen kommen,
und alle deine kleinen
– sie kommen aus dem Kopfe –
sind sie nicht alle *schlecht* gedacht?

85.

Sei eine Platte von Gold –
so werden sich die Dinge auf dir
in goldener Schrift einzeichnen.

86.

Rechtschaffen steht er da,
mit mehr Sinn für das Rechte
in seiner linksten Zehe,
als mir im ganzen Kopfe sitzt:
ein Tugend-Untier,
weißbemäntelt.

83.

Be easy on what has such tender skin!
Why would you scrape the
down from such things?

84.

Your great thoughts,
they come from your heart
and all your small ones
– they come from your head –
are they not all badly thought?

85.

Be a plate of gold,
so all things will bed
drawn on you in golden script.

86.

Upright, he stands there,
with more righteousness
in his left toe
than sits in my whole head –
a virtuous beast,
in a white cloak.

87.

Schon ahmt er sich selber nach,
schon ward er müde,
schon sucht er die Wege, die er ging –
und jüngst noch liebte er alles *Unbegangne*!

....

heimlich verbrannt,
nicht für seinen Glauben.
vielmehr daß er zu keinem Glauben
den Mut mehr fand.

88.

Wie sicher ist dem Unsteten auch
ein Gefängnis!
Wie ruhig schlafen die Seelen
eingefangner Verbrecher!
Am Gewissen leiden nur
Gewissenhafte!

89.

Zu lange saß er im Käfig,
dieser Entlaufne!
Zu lange fürchtete er einen
Stockmeister!
Furchtsam geht er nun seines Wegs:
Alles macht ihn stolpern,
der Schatten eines Stocks schon macht ihn stolpern.

87.

Already he gauges himself,
already he becomes tired
already he searches the way he had gone –
and, still young, he loved everything *unlimited*!

....

secretly burned,
not for his faith,
rather, he found more
courage not to believe!

88.

How safe is a prison
for the restless!
How peacefully sleep the souls of
prison breakers!
From conscience suffers only the
conscientious!

89.

He sat too long in a cage,
this runaway!
Too long he feared
a jailer!
He is frightened to go on his way:
Everything makes him stumble,
the shadow of the jail already makes him trip.

90.

Ihr Rauchkammern und verdumpften Stuben,
ihr Käfige und engen Herzen,
wie wolltet ihr freien Geistes sein!

91.

Was hilft's! Sein Herz
ist eng und all sein Geist
ist in diesen engen Käfig
eingefangen, eingeklemmt.

92.

Enge Seelen,
Krämerseelen!
Wenn das Geld in den Kasten springt,
springt die Seele immer mit hinein!

93.

Die Sträflinge des Reichtums,
deren Gedanken kalt wie Ketten klirren,
– sie erfanden sich die heiligste Langeweile
und die Begierde nach Mond- und Werkeltagen.

90.

Your smoky rooms and damp chambers,
your cages and narrow hearts,
how could you be free spirits!

91.

What can help? His heart
is narrow and his spirit
is in a narrow cage,
imprisoned, squeezed.

92.

Narrow souls,
shopkeepers' souls!
When money jumps into the till,
their souls always jump in along with it.

93.

The convicts of wealth,
whose thoughts bite cold like a chain –
– they invented for themselves a holy boredom
and the passion for moon- and working days.

94.

Bei bedecktem Himmel,
wenn man Pfeile und tötende Gedanken
nach seinen Feinden schießt,
da verleumdeten sie den Glücklichen.
....
Mein Glück macht ihnen Wehe:
diesen Neidbolden ward mein Glück zum Schatten;
sie frösteln bei sich: blicken grün dazu –

95.

Sie lieben ach! und werden nicht geliebt,
sie zerfleischen sich selber,
weil niemand sie umarmen will.
....
Sie verlernten Fleisch essen,
mit Weihlein spielen,
– sie härmten sich über die Maßen.

96.

Seid ihr Weiber,
daß ihr an dem, was ihr liebt,
leiden wollt?

94.

Amid cloudly skies,
if you shoot arrows and deadly thoughts
At your enemies,
you slander fortune.
....
My happiness makes them suffer:
their jealousy shadows my happiness;
they shiver near me: and look green –

95.

They love . . . ah! and are not loved,
they tear themselves to pieces,
because nobody will hug them.
....
They unlearned how to eat meat,
to play with women,
– they grieved over this restraint.

96.

Are you the woman
who wants to
suffer for your love?

97.

Milch fließt
in ihrer Seele; aber wehe!
ihr Geist ist molkicht.

98.

Ihre Kälte
macht meine Erinnrung erstarren?
Habe ich je dies Herz
an mir glühn und klopfen gefühlt?

99.

Sie sind kalt, diese Gelehrten!
Daß ein Blitz in ihre Speise schlüge
und ihre Mäuler lernten Feuer fressen?

100.

Ihr Sinn ist ein Widersinn,
ihr Witz ist ein Doch- und Aber-Witz.

97.

Milk flows
in her soul; but woe!
her spirit is milked.

98.

Their coldness
makes my memory rigid?
Have I ever felt this heart
red hot and beating?

99.

They are cold, these learned ones!
Will lightning strike their food and
will their mouths learn to eat fire?

100.

Your mind is a contradiction,
your wit is a Yet and However-wit.

101.

Eure falsche Liebe
zum Vergangnen,
eine Totengräberliehe –,
sie ist ein Raub am Leben:
ihr stehlt sie der Zukunft ab.

....

Ein Gelehrter *alter* Dinge:
ein Totengräber-Handwerk,
ein Leben zwischen Särgen und Sägespänen!

102.

O diese Dichter!
Hengste sind unter ihnen,
die auf eine keusche Weise wiehern.

103.

Der Dichter, der lügen kann
wissentlich, willentlich,
der kann allein Wahrheit reden.

104.

Unsre Jagd nach der Wahrheit –
ist sie eine Jagd nach Glück?

101.

Your false love
of the past,
a grave digger's love –
she is a robber of life:
she steals the future from you.
....
A scholar of *old* things:
a grave digger's handy work,
a life, between coffins and sawdust!

102.

Oh, these poets!
There are steeds amongst
them, neighing upon a way of chastity.

103.

The poet, who can
willingly and knowingly lie,
can alone tell the truth.

104.

Our hunt toward truth –
is it a hunt after happiness?

105.

Die Wahrheit –
ein Weib, nichts Besseres:
arglistig in ihrer Scham:
was sie am liebsten möchte,
sie will's nicht wissen,
sie hält die Finger vor . . .
Wem gibt sie nach? Der Gewalt allein! –
So braucht Gewalt,
seid hart, ihr Weisesten!
Ihr müßt sie zwingen,
die verschämte Wahrheit . . .
Zu ihrer Seligkeit
braucht's des Zwanges –
– sie ist ein Weib, nichts Besseres.

106.

Wir dachten übel voneinander? . . .
Wir waren uns zu fern.
Aber nun, in dieser kleinsten Hütte,
angepflockt an *ein* Schicksal,
wie sollten wir uns noch feind sein?
Man muß sich schon lieben,
wenn man sich nicht entlaufen kann.

105.

The truth –
a woman, nothing better:
deceitful in her shame:
what she loves most,
she does not want to know,
she spreads out her fingers . . .
to whom will she surrender? Power alone! –
You need to be forceful,
be hard you wise ones!
You must force her,
the shameless truth . . .
With her sanctity,
force is necessary
– she is a woman, nothing better.

106.

We thought badly of each other? . . .
We were too far apart.
But now, in this small hut,
tied together in *one* fate,
how could we be enemies?
One must love oneself already,
When one cannot run away.

107.

'Liebe den Feind,
laß dich rauben von dem Räuber':
das Weib hört's und – tut's.

108.

Wem ziemt die Schönheit?
Dem Manne nicht:
den Mann *versteckt* die Schönheit, –
aber wenig taugt ein versteckter Mann.
Tritt frei herfür –

109.

Der schönste Leib – – ein Schleier nur,
In den sich schamhaft – Schönres hüllt.

110.

Ein vornehmes Auge
mit Samtvorhängen:
selten hell, –
es ehrt den, dem es sich offen zeigt.

107.

'Love thy enemy,
let the robber rob you':
The woman hears – – and obeys.

108.

Beauty is proper for whom?
Not the man:
the man *hides* his beauty –
but a hidden man is of little use.
Stand out freely –

109.

The loveliest body – – only a bashful veil
in which a beautiful woman wraps herself.

110.

A distinguished eye
with velvet curtains:
seldom bright –
it honors when it opens itself.

111.

Langsame Augen,
welche selten lieben:
aber wenn sie lieben, blitzt es herauf
wie aus Goldschächten,
wo ein Drache am Hort der Liebe wacht . . .

112.

(Der Widerspenstige –)
schlecht mit sich selber
verheiratet, unfreundlich,
sein eigener Hausdrache.

113.

Schon wird er unwirsch
zackicht reckt
er die Ellenbogen;
seine Stimme versauert sich,
sein Auge blickt Grünspan.

114.

Der Himinel steht in Flammen,
das Meer fletscht die Zähne
gehen dich – das Meer
speit nach uns!

111.

Slow eyes,
which seldom love:
but when they love, it is
like a bolt from golden shafts
where a dragon guards the hoard of love . . .

112.

(The willful –)
married to himself
in a bad way, unfriendly,
he is his own house dragon.

113.

Already he becomes surly,
he points
his elbows outwards;
his voice sours itself,
his eyes glint *verdigris*.[10]

114.

The sky is in flames,
the sea grinds her teeth
against you – the sea
spits at us!

115.

So spricht jeder Feldherr:
'Gib weder dem Sieger
noch dem Besiegten Ruhe!'
....
ein Reisender in Waffen,
ungeduldig,
daß jemand ihn aufhalten könnte.

116.

'Auch der Rauch ist zu etwas nütz',
so spricht der Beduine, ich spreche es mit:
du Rauch, kündest du nicht
dem, der unterwegs ist,
die Nähe eines gastfreundlichen Herds?
....
ein müder Wanderer –
den mit hartem Gebell
ein Hund empfängt.

117.

Das sind Krebse, mit denen habe ich kein Mitgefühl:
greifst du sie, so kneipen sie;
läßt du sie, geht's rückwärts.

115.

So speaks every field sentry:
'Give peace to
neither victor, nor vanquished!'
....
a trafficker in weapons –
impatient,
that someone might detain him.

116.

'The smoke too has his uses', so
speaks the Beduine – I speak with it:
you smoke – will you not show a
wanderer the vicinity of a
friendly hearth for guests?
....
a tired wanderer – – –
welcomed by the
loud bark of a dog.

117.

There are crabs, with whom I have little feeling:
you touch them, they pinch;
you let them go, they scuttle backwards.

118.

Ein glitzernder tanzender Bach, den
ein krummes Bett
von Felsen einfing:
was macht ihn wieder frei?
Zwischen schwarzen Steinen
glänzt und zuckt seine Ungeduld.

119.

Krumm gehn große Menschen und Ströme,
krumm, aber zu *ihrem* Ziele:
das ist ihr bester Mut,
sie fürchten sich vor krummen Wegen nicht.

120.

Jenseits des Nordens, des Eises, des Heute,
jenseits des Todes,
abseits:
unser Leben, *unser* Glück!
Weder zu Lande,
noch zu Wasser
kannst du den Weg
zu den Hyperboreern finden:
von *uns* wahrsagte so ein weiser Mund.

118.

A glittering, dancing brook,
caught by a crooked
bed of rocks:
how can it free itself?
Between black rocks, it
glitters and twitches its impatience.

119.

Crooked go great men and streams,
crooked, but to their destination:
that is their best courage,
they are not afraid of the crooked path.

120.

Beyond the north, ice and today,
beyond death,
out of the way:
our life, our luck!
Neither on land,
nor on water
can you find the way
to the Hyperborean:[11]
a wise mouth foretold us.

121.

Willst du sie fangen?
Rede ihnen zu
als verirrten Schafen:
'Euren Weg, o euren Weg,
ihr habt ihn verloren!'
Sie folgen jedem nach,
der so ihnen schmeichelt.
'Wie? hatten wir einen Weg?' –
reden sie zu sich heimlich:
'es scheint wirklich, wir haben einen Weg!'

122.

Nacht ist's: wieder über den Dächern
wandelt des Mondes feistes Antlitz.
Er, der eifersüchtigste aller Kater,
allen Liebenden blickt er eifersüchtig,
dieser blasse, fette 'Mann im Monde'.
Lüstern schleicht er um alle dunklen Ecken,
lehnt breit sich in halbverschlossene Fenster,
einem lüsternen, fetten Mönche gleich
geht frech er nachts auf verbotnen Wegen.

121.

Will you catch them?
Speak to them,
these lost sheep:
'Your way, your way,
You have lost it!'
They will follow anyone
who flatters them.
'What? Did we have a path?' –
They speak in secrecy:
'It is clear that we have a path!'

122.

It is night: again over the roofs,
wanders the fat face of the moon.
He, the most jealous of all cats,
looks jealously at all lovers,
this pale, fat 'man in the moon'.
He creeps around all dark corners,
leans far into half open windows,
like a lecherous, fat monk, he travels
cheekily upon nightly forbidden paths.

Der Einsamste

Nun, da der Tag
des Tages müde ward, und aller Sehnsucht Bäche
von neuem Trost plätschern,
auch alle Himmel, aufgehängt in Gold-Spinnetzen,
zu jeden Müden sprechen: 'ruhe nun!' –
was ruhst du nicht, du dunkles Herz,
was stachelt dich zu fußwunder Flucht . . .
wes harrest du?

Fleiß und Genie

Dem Fleißigen neid ich seinen Fleiß:
goldhell und gleich fließt ihm der Tag herauf,
goldhell und gleich zurück,
hinab ins dunkle Meer, –
und um sein Lager blüht
Vergessen, gliederlösendes.

Das Honig-Opfer

Bringt Honig mir, eis-frischen Waben-Honig!
Mit Honig opfr' ich allem, was da schenkt,
was gönnt, was gütig ist –: erhebt die Herzen!

The loneliest

Now that the day
becomes tired of the day, and all longing brooks
splash with new comfort,
the sky hangs upon golden-spider webs,
all the tired ones speak: 'Rest now!' –
why do you not rest, you dark heart,
what ties you to your flight . . .
why do you hesitate?

Diligence and genius

I envy the diligence of the diligent:
golden and like, the day flows upon him,
golden and straight
away back, down into the dark sea,
around his camp,
forgotten, limbless.

The honey sacrifice

Bring honey for me, ice-fresh honey comb!
With honey, I sacrifice honey to all that gives,
that enjoys, that is kind –: lift up your hearts!

Das eherne Schweigen

Fünf Ohren – und kein Ton darin!
Die Welt ward stumm . . .

Ich horchte mit dem Ohr meiner *Neugierde*:
fünfmal warf ich die Angel über mich,
fünfmal zog ich keinen Fisch herauf. –
Ich fragte, – keine Antwort lief mir ins Netz . . .

Ich horchte mit dem Ohr meiner *Liebe* –

The brazen silence

Five ears – and no sound therein!
The world became silent . . .

I listened with the ear of my *curiosity*:
five times, I cast my fishing rod,
five times, I did not catch a fish. –
I asked – no reply swam into my net . . .

I listen with the ears of my *love* –

NOTES

1 This is most likely an allusion to a similar formulations in Ovid, such as in his *The Loves*, Book II, Elegy VI, where he laments the death of a parrot ('a faithful friend') he had given to his lover,

> plena fuit vobis omni concordia vita,
> et stetit ad finem longa tenaxque fides.

Incidentally, the structure and the thematic content, that of love, is also the same as Nietzsche's love letter.

2 Saalek is a castle in East Prussia.

3 A chamois is a goat-antelope that is native to the Alps and to other mountain ranges throughout Europe.

4 Chadsche Schams al-Din Mohammad Hafes′e Schirazi (1319–89). Legendary Persian poet and Sufi who was popularized by Goethe in the romantic period. There are strong affinities between the life of Nietzsche and Hafis, including the untimely death of their fathers. The reference to wine alludes to his allusions to the 'goblet of love' and his home region of Shiraz.

5 In *Dandayamana Janushirasana* yoga, the standing head to knee pose is undertaken to develop patience, but it is unclear if this was intended by Nietzsche.

6 On the one hand, Larifari may refer to the practise of nonsense verse set to music in the manner of Guido of Arezzo, a Benedictine monk and music teacher. On the other hand, Larifari was the ambiguous anti-hero character in the puppet plays of Franz Graf von Pocci, a German musician and writer.

7 'First to write, then to philosophize!'

8 The 'Dog Star', or *Sirius*, is the brightest star in the sky, and the main star in the constellation *Canis major*, or 'Big Dog'.

It is associated with the heat of summer, in the sense of the 'dog days' of summer.

9 The 'Gemini Jewel' is an exotic, tropical orchid that resembles both the nether parts of a woman and a tutu.

10 *Verdigris* is the weathering of bronze, usually near the sea; at the same time, *verdigris* was used by artists throughout history as a green pigment.

11 *Hyperborean* is an allusion to the North, and to the North wind, expressed in the mythology of ancient Greece, in the mythical image of a people who lived to the north of Thrace.